‹ *Roy Vernon Sowers* ›

A LIFE IN RARE BOOKS

‹ *Roy Vernon Sowers* ›

A LIFE IN RARE BOOKS

Roger Burford Mason

Subway Books, Toronto, 1997

ISBN 0-9681660-4-0

Published by Subway Books Ltd,
247 Albany Avenue, Toronto, Ontario, Canada M5R 3C7.
Fax (416) 538-3317.

Typeset in Galliard, printed on Zephyr Antique Laid, and bound at
The Porcupine's Quill Inc.

1 2 3 4 • 99 98 97

‹ *Contents* ›

‹ *Acknowledgements* ›

The author wishes to thank the large number of people who provided help, advice and guidance, including staff of the University of Toronto archives and of the libraries of the University of California at Santa Cruz, Berkeley, Davis and San Francisco – in particular, Carol Champion at UC Santa Cruz. I should also like to single out persons at other institutions: Jill Cogen, reference librarian at the Huntington; W. Glen Curnoe at the London [Ontario] Public Library; Carolyn Garner at the Pasadena Public Library; Clive Hurst at the Bodleian in Oxford; David Kotin, special collections librarian at the Metropolitan Toronto Central Reference Library; Asa Peavy, special collections librarian at the San Francisco Public Libraries; Sara Timby at the Stanford University Library; and Bruce Whiteman at the Clark Library, UCLA. Many of Sowers's friends and colleagues in the rare-book trade were also most helpful: Charles Antin, New York; Muir Dawson, Los Angeles; Donald C. Dickinson, Tucson; and Bernard M. Rosenthal, Berkeley. A particular word of thanks to Richard Press of Sacramento who lent me – a complete stranger, importuning him from Canada by email – his own very valuable collection of Sowers catalogues. Also, thanks to Ann Whipple of the Book Club of California; Rudolf Bikkers of Toronto; Dale Fetherling of San Diego; Joanne Shurvell, formerly of Oxford University Press, Toronto; and Daniel Williman of Binghamton University. And finally, as always, my gratitude to my wife, Aileen Burford Mason, whose continued belief in my writing is as staunch as her support for it.

Sower's children, Anthony and Lucia, helped enormously in bringing their father to life by lending documents and photographs.

MR. R. V. SOWERS of the DON QUIXOTE BOOK SHOP invites you to the Opening of his New Gallery and Shop at 90 King Street West, on Thursday Evening, Nov. 5th. There will be an Exhibiton of Original Etchings & Block Prints by the SOCIETY OF CANADIAN PAINTER-ETCHERS.

The Exhibition remains during November

‹ *Canada* ›

IN RESEARCHING SOMEONE whose life was rich, but who lived in relative obscurity and died more than twenty-five years ago (and whose spouse had also died before I began this project), I found that a lot of trails were cold and others led nowhere. So I am surprised that I was able to draw together as much information as I have about the antiquarian bookseller Roy Vernon Sowers. Yet all the while I have remained profoundly conscious of the fact that, in many respects, what I have turned up has not been enough for me to be able to claim this as a biography. Rather, what I have written is an appreciation of someone who, at the time of his death in 1970, was already a member of an obsolescent breed – the educated, opinionated, bibliophile and scholarly book and print dealer. If this modest book serves as a study of the life and work of one man alone, it also serves as a memorial to that brotherhood, which he graced for more than forty years. I never met Sowers, but being familiar with the fraternity in general makes me believe that in some ways I was acquainted with him specifically.

From 1977 until 1988, when I emigrated to Toronto from England, I edited and published a quarterly journal, *Albion*, which celebrated the old craft of letterpress printing. In the early 1970s, I had acquired some old printing equipment and type in order to publish pamphlets of poetry and monographs about printing. With the high purpose of the newly converted I then founded *Albion* as a magazine of printing and publishing history, because at that time there was no regular periodical devoted to these passions of mine. One of our subscribers was Dr Edmund E. Simpson, now alas deceased, who lived in the foothills of the Sierra Nevada, east of Sacramento, in Placerville, California (which he often spoke of affectionately by its Gold

Rush name, Old Hangtown). As well as being an *Albion* subscriber, Ed was one of a shadowy international band of Luddites like myself who, in the teeth of new printing technologies that could churn out many thousands of impressions an hour, persisted in finding everything about letterpress printing fascinating, deliberate and beautiful. Like me, Ed had his own printing shop at home; his was equipped with a Chandler & Price treadle press and an enviable array of typefaces. From this shop, which he called the Blackwood Press, he sent to his friends a steady stream of beautifully printed pamphlets and ephemera, illustrated with his own elegant woodcuts.

I corresponded with Ed for several years, and had the pleasure of calling on him at his mountain home in the summer of 1984. During that visit he gave me, as a memento, a pamphlet he had printed in 1980 entitled *An Excerpt from the Book Catalogues of Roy Vernon Sowers*. I read and enjoyed Ed's personal reminiscence of this remarkable antiquarian book dealer, whose catalogues were the delight of all who received them. But then *An Excerpt* disappeared onto my bookshelves and did not see the light of day again until recently, when I came on it by accident while looking for something else.

I knew that Ed had trained as a doctor at McGill University in Montreal and had pleasant memories of his time in Canada. Now, as I reread his tribute to Sowers, I was reminded that Sowers had come from Ontario originally (although he lived most of his adult life in California and came to regard himself as an American). I knew I had found someone about whom I needed to learn more. This is what I discovered ...

The distance between the quiet order of London, Ontario, and the big-city excitement of San Francisco is great, but not greater than the distance one might plot between the dreams of a working-class boy, beguiled by books but able to afford only the ones on the remainder table at his local bookstore, and the hard-won success of a world-renowned scholar and antiquarian book dealer, whose stock was worth hundreds of thousands of US dollars when he relinquished it in 1969. That the man in question, Roy Vernon Sowers, became respected in the book world for his wisdom and wit, and his profound knowledge of the trade, attests to the fact that such a long and unusual journey was not undertaken lightly nor pursued frivolously or selfishly.

Roy Vernon Sowers – he neither used nor permitted any abbreviation of his name – was born in southwestern Ontario, probably at the farm of his paternal grandparents near Brantford, on 7 August 1897. Brantford city directories list a number of people by the name of Sowers at the turn of the century, including the subject's father, Herbert R. Sowers, although the directories for London show that Roy Vernon Sowers's family was living at 447 Woodland Avenue in London the year he was born.

In an unpublished memoir (lent me by his son) Roy Vernon Sowers remembered that his 'father was earning six dollars a week as an apprentice candy maker in a London factory. Much later he rose to foreman status, but I think he never in his life received more than forty dollars a week ... Ten hours a day, six days a week he worked ... When he died, worn out, I think that simple home was almost paid for.'

The Sowerses are first recorded in the directories in 1843; in the year of Roy Vernon's birth, his father is listed as a confectioner on Dundas Street. His mother, Emma F. Sowers, had been a Dawson, another old-time London family, and Roy Vernon was to have two brothers: Herbert, born two years after him, who died while still a young man; and Harold, the youngest by several years, who became a salesman and lived with his parents at Woodland Avenue for at least part of his adult life. The family home was in a row of solid lower-middle-class houses, somewhat to the east of the city core, a mile or more's walk from the candy store, which was at 601/2 Dundas Street, in London's main shopping area. The house was demolished and replaced by one larger in 1939, but Woodland Avenue is still a quiet residential street; the candy store has long been lost to the inevitable redevelopment that turned over the old city to expensive apartments, antiseptic banks and the headquarters of the insurance companies with which, to Ontarians, London is virtually synonymous.

When he became old enough, Roy had to augment the family income with a newspaper route and by errands for a local store. In the summers, he also worked on his grandparents' farm, a time he was to remember in the introductory essay to one of his book catalogues forty or more years later. In that self-revealing introduction to Catalogue Fifty, written at his hilltop fruit farm and book-room in the Santa Cruz mountains, probably in the autumn of 1953, Sowers remembered his Ontario childhood with nostalgic affection: 'I write this in the midst of a spell of Indian Summer, reminiscent of the eastern autumns I used to know. The pear trees and the vineyards begin to show the brilliant colours due to occasional frosty nights. I see in my mind's eye the blaze of maples familiar to my boyhood in Ontario and again I sway in the tops of the supple hickories, while the nuts go clattering down. How long is it, I wonder, since I have tasted a crisp snow-apple, picked from the tree on a frosty November afternoon?' In this poetic vein, he continues his introduction to the books in his catalogue, musing about great men, great ideas and the great books they have engendered, but he ends with a characteristically self-deflating remark: 'Let us pour a little libation to the dreams of great men of other days; and may the good Lord forgive me for selling these things for money!'

Sowers developed an early love of books by reading (among his favourites) G.A. Henty, Rudyard Kipling, Sir Walter Scott and Mark Twain: all the usual names for a young person of his time and place. In later years he recalled that he scoured the bookstores of London and surrounding towns in the evenings and on weekends and borrowed books six at a time from the London Public Library. Of his youthful literary enthusiasms, he wrote, 'I still have the attractive little volumes published by the Foulis Press of Edinburgh, which I picked up for ten cents, but it never occurred to me to investigate the thousands of other volumes on the lofty shelves of those shops.'

Until 1917, Sowers attended London Collegiate Institute; then he entered University College at the University of Toronto to study political economy. He was twenty. The university's Roll of Service for the Great War notes that he enlisted in the university flying corps cadet unit in 1917 and trained as a flight mechanic. The flying corps was where the glamour and glory were. His cadet identity photograph shows a dark-haired, slim fellow with a lively, interested face, while the more formal class photographs from the same period suggest him to be polished and confident-looking, quite at ease in his cap and gown. Sowers's academic record was sound rather than exciting. His grades in English, French, history and some compulsory sciences were average, or a little above, but not the stuff of academic excellence, and certainly not suggestive of the tremendous scholarly authority in which he was to cloak himself in later years. Nevertheless he was clearly an adequate student, and a popular one, for he was elected president of his class in 1920. On Sunday afternoons, he recorded in his memoir, he worked 'as a sort of guard in charge of the art collection at The Grange [now the Art Gallery of Ontario]. The curator was Edward R. Greig, a Canadian and a gentleman [and the person] who first put into my head the idea of going to Oxford after graduation [and then] loaned me the money to do it.'

Sowers threw himself into various aspects of university journalism. For most of his time as an undergraduate, he wrote for the university newspaper, the *Varsity*, using the pseudonym Don Quixote, a choice that was to recur some years later when he opened a Toronto bookstore with that name. He was the founding editor of the University College literary journal, *Patches*, in 1920, and its editor-in-chief in 1921, his graduation year. He was also editor-in-chief of *Torontonensis*, the university yearbook, for 1920-21. The anonymous compiler of the brief biographical note about him in *Torontonensis* recorded that Sowers had listed his passions as 'life insurance and journalism.' The writer concluded dryly, 'Scribbling will be the ruin of him.' In fact, the opposite would be true. What attracted people to him all his life were his ideas and his writing. The New York book collector Charles Antin, in an article in *AB Bookman's Weekly* in February 1984, recalled receiving his first Sowers catalogue in 1961 and being struck by 'his unusually well-written and entertaining foreword entitled "A few thoughts on solitude". From the first moment I read the words, they had an emotional claim on me difficult to describe.' Rose Macaulay, the novelist of the 1920s and 1930s, knew what he meant. Writing about book dealers' catalogues generally, in a collection of essays entitled *Personal Pleasures*, she noted: 'To read these catalogues is like drinking wine in the middle of the morning; it elevates one into that felicitous intoxication in which one feels capable of anything. I must control myself and not write to booksellers in haste … I will wait until the effects are worn off, and then write a postcard sober, temperate, moderate, brief, restrained … But while I wait, those more intemperate than myself will have rushed in and bought … It is obvious that I cannot wait. Probably I should telephone …' Because of their intelligent, pungent and frequently arcane or erudite introductions, not to mention the wide-ranging nature of the books and prints offered, and the elegant and informative notes he provided for many of them, Sowers's catalogues must have been greeted with something of Macaulay's breathless eagerness whenever they appeared. Of the ones Antin received for a number of years, he went on to comment that Sowers's 'descriptions, authoritative as he could make them, were enriched with the warmth of a generous personality. He was a jaunty iconoclast, a person who could not resist giving his candid, outspoken opinion. But what always shined through was an unequivocal love of books.'

All of this was still to come. Sowers graduated from the University of Toronto with a BA in political science and, rather than try to find work immediately, sailed for England in the early autumn in time to study at St Johns College, Oxford, for the Michaelmas Term. This decision, incidentally, would enable him, several years later, to style himself to a Los Angeles newspaper reporter, 'Roy Vernon Sowers, of the University of Toronto, Oxford, and now of the Huntington Library …' Having already developed a passion for books, he may have wished to read for a BA in English Literature at Oxford. According to his own account, he studied economics, but no records exist to verify (or contradict) this. What is known is he did not last out the course, and left before the end of his first academic year.

Decades later he cited lack of funds to explain his abrupt departure, but he never forgot his experiences there. He returned often when on book-buying visits to England and the Continent, and he made a major bequest to the university's famous Bodleian Library.

Although lack of money may well have been the reason he left Oxford early, Sowers nevertheless found funds enough to travel in Europe, where he visited a number of great university and private libraries. In Germany, which was still suffering from the economic effects of the huge reparations extracted by the Allies after the war, he experienced the ravages of inflation and saw the poverty and despair of the German people as they struggled to manage in a world where thousands of Deutschmarks would scarcely buy even a loaf of bread: an experience he never forgot. He managed to write and sell some articles about life in Europe to the Toronto *Evening Telegram*, whose modest payments must have helped him keep travelling until he was forced to return late in 1922.

Sowers came home to a depressed economy, and to survive he led a varied existence. For some time he sold books door to door, trudging around the farms of northern Alberta with a heavy home compendium, a combined medical, cookery and veterinary book. He met with limited success, and returned to Toronto, where, for several months, he sold Haldeman-Julius Little Blue Books through the post. Until finally closed down by the FBI in the 1950s, the Haldeman-Julius Company of Girard, Kansas, was one of the most extraordinary educational institutions in American history. For five cents (only twice the cost of a metropolitan daily newspaper) it sold little blue-covered paperbound books, about three-and-a-half by five inches, covering hundreds of novelists, essayists, philosophers and social critics with ties to the progressive movement in politics or the avant-garde in art: Havelock Ellis, D.H. Lawrence, Bertrand Russell, Upton Sinclair. The crude little booklets sold literally millions and millions of copies, and taught generations of Americans about forbidden subjects such as sex, socialism and poetry. In its mass reach, the Haldeman-Julius firm was therefore fundamentally different from the sort of populist publishing of canonical works being pursued in Britain at approximately the same period: the shilling editions, uniformly bound, in series such as Routledge's Universal Classics, Dent's Everyman's Library or Grant Richards's World Classics (the last of these later taken over by the Oxford University Press); the 6d Penguins would not arrive until the middle 1930s. How starved for reading people were, Sowers commented of that time, as orders came in from all over, including some from above the Arctic Circle.

Among the many jobs Sowers tried during this period was one as a reporter at the Toronto *Daily Star*, which he called in his manuscript memoir 'one of the most sensational newspapers' of the day. According to Charles Antin – who had the advantage of speaking with the widow, Margaret Sowers, in the early 1980s – Sowers was, in his own words, 'fired for refusing to cover a murder.' He taught school briefly as well. Also, he sold a product he may long have thought of selling, given what his university colleague wrote in *Torontonensis*: insurance. Whatever the truth might have been, an information card that Sowers returned to the University of Toronto's alumni registry, dated 22 May 1923, lists his address as 6331/2 Spadina Avenue and his occupation as agent of the Canada Life Assurance Company, City Branch. Yet by the middle 1920s he is recorded in the Toronto city directories as a bookseller and also as the general manager of Academy Publications. I could find no trace of that imprint in professional directories or the trade press, and no evidence of any publications under such a name. The only other surviving reference to Academy Publications is a sample of the letterhead Sowers used at that time; below the deck, it carries the phrase 'The Ten Cent Classics.' Sowers was selling the Haldeman-Julius titles at twice their American price, advertising them through the *Family Herald* of Montreal.

Sowers's Toronto bookstore is an even more important mystery. The Don Quixote Book Shop was located at a number of different places in the bustling downtown area between 1924 and 1927, and he had a friend, Morley Ayearst, design a logo for it – Don Quixote tilting at a windmill. Unfortunately, virtually nothing about the shop can be learned at this late date, beyond what Sowers set down in his unpublished reminiscences. Sowers remembered the first store as an eighty-dollar-a-month hole-in-the-wall in the financial district, about eight feet wide and thirty deep, with one window at the front and the only entrance at the side. Sowers 'had the interior painted a sort of tax-cab orange colour which, despite the glare, did succeed in overcoming the dinginess of the place. Then I spread out my stock of new books, the Haldeman-Julius pamphlets and a lot of literary magazines, and opened for business.' In time, he took an employee, a young Englishman named Harry Bendle. 'Since I was open always every night, a number of would-be Bohemians frequented the sort, and at eleven or twelve several of us would repair to Child's [on Bay Street] for coffee, to watch pancakes being tossed in the window, and to carry on our literary conversations.'

After vigorous enquiry, I could find no one alive who claimed to have patronized the Don Quixote, nor any mention of it in the book-trade publications of the time. The James Collection of 1920s Toronto streetscapes and other photographic images at the City of Toronto Archives holds no picture of the appropriate city blocks at the period when the Don Quixote was in business on them. As close as I could come to a breakthrough was to learn from Robert Stacey, the art historian, that he believes his grandfather, the artist C.W. Jefferys, frequented the Don Quixote. If so, Jefferys was probably the representative customer. For one truth we know from Sowers's own pen is that he modelled it on some of the so-called modern bookstores he would have visited in England, whose stock, a mixture of new and used books, attracted local writers, artists and bohemians. Specifically, Sowers mentions Sylvia Beach's Shakespeare and Company in Paris and two New York stores, Madge Jenison's Sunwise Turn and Byrne Hackett's Brick Row Books. The biggest influence on Sowers, however, was Harold Monro's Poetry Book Shop in London, which he would have visited, for it was a real bookman's bookshop, trading in the most modern authors of poetry, novels and ideas. It was in Devonshire Street, just off Theobalds Road, 'in the heart of London, five minutes' walk away from the British Museum,' as the shop's first prospectus declared. Writing in T.S. Eliot's *Criterion* in July 1932, F.S. Flint, the English poet and critic and one of the parents of Imagism, described the Poetry Book Shop's origins: 'Monro was lamenting the depressed state of English poetry to Beerbohm Tree and was challenged, 'If you feel that, why on Earth don't you do something?' Monro went and did something; he spent the rest of his life and a great deal of his money doing it.'

Monro also played a significant part in promoting the poetry of Edward Marsh, W.H. Davies, Robert Frost, Walter de la Mare and Rupert Brooke, and he edited and produced important anthologies of the so-called Georgians. His blind spot was the moderns. Monro holds the unfortunate distinction of having turned down, in 1914, Eliot's 'The Love Song of J. Alfred Prufrock' when it was offered by Conrad Aiken, who was trying to use his influence to place the poem for Eliot. Monro referred to it as insane. Nevertheless, Monro published books by Robert Graves, Frances Cornford, Ezra Pound, Richard Aldington, Edith Sitwell, Frances Meynell and Humbert Wolfe. To his lasting credit, he found, published and promoted the poetry of the brilliant and anguished Charlotte Mew. Sowers would surely have carried many books from Monro's list, given his own particular interest in the Georgians, who formed, in 1929, a substantial part of the first catalogue he issued as a rare book dealer from California. We know from the same source, which obviously drew on his stock from Toronto, that Sowers stocked intellectual and artistic magazines such as Gordon Craig's *Mask* and perhaps the important English review the *Dial*, as well as the magazines edited by Monro himself: the *Chapbook*, *Poetry Review*, *Georgian Poetry* and *Poetry and Drama*. Equally influential was Harriet Monroe's *Poetry: A Magazine of Verse* (popularly known as *Poetry Chicago*), in which W.W.E. Ross, Canada's first true modernist poet, was published regularly (and in which the rejected 'Prufrock' eventually found its home).

Sowers would write that Bendle and he 'always had time to talk to anyone who dropped in to spend an hour' at the Don Quixote. 'There I first participated in those long discussions in which the young still indulge, about the 'Ideal Bookshop'; then, as now, this always involved easy chairs, tables, undisturbed browsing at will, and preferably tea or coffee. Someone who really wanted to buy a book might well hesitate to interrupt such serious discussion, even if he penetrated the wall of cigarette smoke. As I scorned best sellers, I got only the fringe of the new books trade; collectors, American and Canadian, periodically emptied my shelves of books ... Assuming that all booklovers were *ipso facto* virtuous, I gave credit to anyone, and of course many of these accounts were never paid.'

Along with some new books and some of antiquarian interest, his inventory of contemporary literature would have reflected what was then considered the *dernier cri* of desirable modern books and authors. The fact that we know almost nothing about the Don Quixote, however, seems to me to symbolise the fact that relatively little primary research has been done into the Canadian literary flowering of the 1920s, which paralleled the dominance of the Group of Seven in the visual arts (who, by comparison, have probably been studied too much). It was in 1925, smack in the middle of the Don Quixote's existence, that Charles G.D. (later Sir Charles G.D.) Roberts returned to Canada after literary careers in London and New York, because there was suddenly sufficient literary infrastructure in Toronto to support (and flatter) him. Consider some of the new Canadian books that Sowers likely would have carried: E.J. Pratt's *Newfoundland Verse* (1923), *The Witches' Brew* (1925) and *The Titans* (1926); Frederick Philip Grove's *Settlers of the Marsh* (1925); and Mazo De la Roche's *Possession* (1923) and *Delight* (1926). Stephen Leacock published *Over the Footlights* in 1923 and *My Discovery of England* in 1926, and Roberts's cousin, Bliss Carman, published frequent poetry collections during the period in question, in addition to co-editing, with Lorne Pierce, the editor of the Ryerson Press and one of the prime movers of this renaissance, *Our Canadian Literature: Representative Verse, English and French* (1922). Another important anthology of the time was *The Voice of Canada*, carefully chosen by A.M. Stephen. Early critical writing about Canadian literature included the poet Lionel Stevenson's *Appraisals of Canadian Literature* (1926), which was widely influential.

ROY VERNON SOWERS

announces

a Series of 10 Lectures on the

HISTORY OF ETCHING AND ENGRAVING

from the 15th Century to Today.

To be held every Thursday, at 3:30 P. M.

Commencing

Thursday, February 5th,

In his Print Room at 1005 East Green Street, Pasadena.

Each Lecture will be illustrated with Original Prints by the Masters under discussion

Tea will be served

✚ ✚ ✚

For convenience sake these meetings are referred to as lectures; but it is intended rather that they shall take the form of informal talks to a small group of interested people.

As the capacity of the room is strictly limited, and over half the seats already booked, those interested are urged to subscribe by return mail.

✚ ✚ ✚

Subscription Price is $10.00 for the Series

Although he was not yet thirty, Sowers was already developing a taste for finely produced books, and his stock most probably would have included the bibelots of the American publisher Thomas Bird Mosher (1852-1923), whose titles Sowers admired immensely and collected, amassing more than a hundred of them over a four-year period.

Mosher, who printed in Portland, Maine, in the first decades of the century, did not begin his career as a provincial publisher until 1891, when he was thirty-nine. He knew that he wanted to produce books of beauty and usefulness, however, and this is exactly what he did, leaving an enduring legacy of collectors' volumes, uniform in their small, elegant format and ranging across the centuries and the artistic and intellectual disciplines, from Marcus Aurelius and Theocritus to Baudelaire to Walter Pater to Whitman. Ten years after Sowers had become a bookseller in Toronto, he wrote in Catalogue Twelve of Mosher's work that the complete set he was offering 'must remain a monument to the impeccable taste of one of our greatest American literary figures … I recommend this set as the foundation of a sound literary education. A work for those who can still read for pleasure.' He did not mention that Mosher – in the days before the United States was a party to the principal copyright conventions – was a pirate, who had the distinction of having illegally copied one of the most famous books of the English typographical renaissance, *The Garland of Rachel*, published by Dr C.O.H. Daniel at his Daniel Press in 1881 and notable for its use of the famous Oxford University Fell types. The text consisted of gift-poems sent to Daniel by friends of the family, including Austin Dobson, John Addington Symonds, Lewis Carroll and Robert Bridges, and was printed for Daniel's infant daughter at his private press at Worcester College in Oxford, where he was a fellow. Mosher printed and published his version of *The Garland* in 1902, and does not seem to have concerned himself with issues of ethics or copyright. Indeed, after he had pirated a copy of a novel by George Meredith, the author wrote him in 1892: 'Sir, a handsome pirate is always half pardoned … I shall receive with pleasure a copy of *Modern Love*, which you have promised to send me.'

Nevertheless, to be published by Mosher was considered something of a coup. As eminent as he was, Robert Frost had hoped to be published by Mosher, but never was. Those who *were* are listed in an admirable bibliography published, appropriately enough, by one of contemporary America's finest private presses, the Gehenna Press of Leonard Baskin, in 1966.

Mosher and Dr Daniel aside, Sowers undoubtedly stocked beautiful and important books from many of the best contemporary fine presses that he had come to admire. From the Nonesuch Press of Francis Meynell in England, he had the wonderful 1925 edition of Robert Burton's *The Anatomy of Melancholy* illustrated by the American book artist McKnight Kauffer: this we know from Sowers's catalogues of a slightly later date. From Harold Curwen's seminal Curwen Press in the East End of London came Ambrose Bierce's *Ten Tales*. Books from Bernard Newdigate's Shakespeare Head Press and Jack Lindsay's Fanfrolico Press, and others from smaller English fine presses such as the Baynard and the Beaumont, and the even smaller Cloister and Vine presses, appear in the same sources. And of course Sowers carried trade books from commercial publishers such as Heinemann, Routledge and Macmillan. I would like to imagine that the Don Quixote is where Canadians went to secure their illicit copies of the Sylvia Beach edition of *Ulysses* (the few who would have been interested at the time).

The most established Canadian cultural publication of the period was the *Literary Digest*, whose cover boasted that it spoke to 'Topics that People of Culture Discuss,' but a fast-rising one was the *Canadian Forum*, which had grown out of the *Rebel*, a University of Toronto literary magazine, in 1920. The *Forum*'s first editor was Barker Fairley, the poet, painter and brilliant Goethe scholar, whose support of the Group of Seven's early works, at the time of their first exhibition at the Art Gallery of Toronto in 1920, helped to establish them. Fairley established the *Forum*'s tradition of encouraging new and emerging Canadian writers, critics, thinkers and radicals. His magazine surely would have been stocked at a bookshop named for Don Quixote, a place that, in the irreducibly provincial city of that time, Sowers was determined should be 'the meeting place of literary Toronto.'

New books by D.H. Lawrence, A.C. Benson, Laurence Binyon, John Galsworthy and so many other disparate types were newly off the presses as Sowers opened the doors of his first bookstore on Richmond Street West in 1924. Still new, still causing excited talk, were Eliot's *The Waste Land*, Aldous Huxley's *Antic Hay* and Bernard Shaw's *Saint Joan* (Sowers would be involved in a production of Shaw's play some years later). Also during Sowers's few years as a bookseller in Toronto, Thomas Mann published *The Magic Mountain*. In 1925 alone, Scott Fitzgerald reached his pinnacle as the chronicler of the jazz age with *The Great Gatsby* and Shaw was awarded the Nobel Prize for Literature: a pair of events that seems to locate the boundaries of the Don Quixote rather neatly. What a time to be a bookseller.

But despite the undoubted quality of his stock, and his enthusiasm as a book-shop owner, Sowers could not make a profit. As he noted many years later, in an article in the *Quarterly News-Letter* of the Book Club of California, 'I was too stupid to price books properly, and learned what most new booksellers learn – that most unsold books very quickly become dead stock, and that publishers' bills inevitably become overdue.'

Sowers must have been happy to be able to return to England in 1925. A report in the *Globe* on 18 June notes that Sowers had been chosen to supervise the Canadian Universities pavilion at the British Empire Exhibition at Wembley, in those days a quiet and leafy London suburb, whose later graceless urbanization the English poet John Betjeman lamented in his long poem 'Metroland.'

London did not detain Sowers long on this occasion, and he was soon back in Toronto in 1925 when he is listed in a business directory as selling books and stationery at 47 Richmond Street West. He added an art gallery to the bookshop to broaden its appeal, a decision that was the harbinger of his expanding interest in graphic art later on. According to the city directories for his latter years in Toronto, Sowers was a seller of fine books and prints as well as manager of the mysterious Academy Publishing Company at 18 Toronto Street.

In the autumn of 1925, according to the Toronto *Daily Star*, Ty Cobb, the legendary baseball player, came down to Toronto from a hunting trip in Northern Ontario with a huge moose, while Tom Mix and Harold Lloyd on film were playing at Toronto's two main cinemas and Shaw's *Candide* was being performed at the Uptown Theatre. On 4 November, auctioneers sold the library of Thomas William Kirby, author of *The Golden Dog*. As an indication of literary taste in the city at that time, a pristine first edition of Catherine Parr Traill's beautiful *Plant Life in Canada* went for fifty cents, whereas a first edition of Washington Irving's *Knickerbocker History of New York* was knocked down for ten dollars. The following day, 5 November, Sowers opened a new version of the Don Quixote at 90 King Street West, boasting a print room, the New Gallery. Here he remained for the rest of his time in Toronto, which wasn't long. Henry Bendle took ill and 'our new location was proving a mistake, and trade had fallen off. Thanks to the prompt loan of an old friend I was saved from bankruptcy ... I struggled with the bookshop for another year or so, and then closed it ... and rather embittered, I left Toronto.'

‹ *Southern California* ›

HEALTH PROBLEMS as well as financial ones influenced Sowers's decision. Troubled with a severe sinus problem for most of his youth and early adulthood, he decided, in 1927, to move to California, where the climate, he thought, would be better for his condition. Furthermore, his growing interest in antiquarian and rare books was leading him to the possibility of a situation at the famous Huntington Library near San Marino, a wealthy district bordering Pasadena in the suburbs of Los Angeles.

Henry E. Huntington, born in Oneonta, New York, in 1850, was the nephew of Collis Potter Huntington, one of the great entrepreneurs in the history of America, whose railway and construction empires made him a multi-millionaire in the latter part of the nineteenth century. Being Collis P. Huntington's nearest relative, Henry worked for his uncle's Central Pacific Railroad for many years, at the same time establishing himself as an astute and acquisitive businessman in his own right. When Collis Huntington died in 1900, Henry inherited his huge wealth, which included a great deal of Southern California real estate, as well as a controlling interest in another railway, the Southern Pacific. In a short time, he sold his uncle's railway interests and used the capital to engage in entrepreneurial schemes and projects of his own, which made him even more enormously wealthy. In time, he had major investments in water, electrical power and land development, and went on to become the largest single landowner in Southern California; he served on as many as sixty companies' boards throughout the country. His particular gift to Southern California was to expand and develop the legendary Pacific Electric Railway Company, establishing the red cars, an efficient inter-urban rail system throughout the burgeoning Los Angeles area. Indeed, it would not be overstating the case to say that, between 1900 and 1910, Henry Huntington's entrepreneurship was largely instrumental in bringing about a tripling of the region's population, as the street railway links he built brought about the wholesale development of adjacent property.

In 1892, Henry Huntington had been en route from New York to join his uncle's railroad company at San Francisco when he visited the extensive estates of J. DeBarth Shorb, who owned a palatial home and grounds in San Marino; the elaborate and exotic gardens alone totalled one hundred and thirty acres. Huntington later bought the property and operated it as a six-hundred-acre ranch (until deciding to sell more than half of it). From about 1903 he had been collecting rare books and art treasures. In 1910, at sixty, he retired from business and began to build an unparalleled private book and art collection, founded on the purchase, for one million dollars, of a library of two thousand volumes from Chatsworth, the ancestral seat of the Dukes of Devonshire. The purchase included twelve folios and thirty-seven quartos of Shakespeare and a collection of printing by William Caxton. In another coup, in 1917, he acquired the Ellesmere manuscript of Chaucer's *Canterbury Tales* when he bought the Bridgewater House Library and Muniments in London; the priceless manuscript is now catalogued as Huntington EL.26.C.9. In building his library, and adding to it an art gallery, Huntington was ably aided by his wife, Arabella Duval Huntington, the widow of his uncle and benefactor, Collis P. Huntington, although the same age as Henry. So it was that, in 1919, the Huntingtons created an endowment of $10.5 million to found the Henry E. Huntington Library, including the main house in the bequest, as well as a Beaux Arts mansion with its great collections of British and French art of the eighteenth and nineteenth centuries, and the wonderful gardens. The Huntington, as it is known familiarly, was intended to be one of America's great cultural facilities, attracting scholars and researchers from around the world. Consequently, it is scarcely to be wondered at that Sowers was impatient to take up the position he had been offered. But having arrived in Pasadena,

Sowers was obliged to wait while the wheels of the library's bureaucracy turned.

While he was waiting, Sowers was offered a job by Alice Millard, the noted Pasadena antiquarian. She also had an interest in prints, fine furniture and *objets d'art*, and she nursed a large and wealthy but not always discerning clientele, to whom she catered with guile and assiduity; for nearly a year, Sowers worked with her at her house, La Miniatura. Millard had been a young teacher in Chicago in her late twenties when she met George Madison Millard at McClurg's, a famous bookstore in that city, where she had gone looking for a biography of William Morris, with whose work and ideas she identified strongly. George Millard was the manager of McClurg's rare-books department, and not only a personal friend of Morris (and of T. J. Cobden-Sanderson) but also a passionate bibliophile, as she was, and a gifted teacher. Although twenty-seven years separated them, they married in 1901, choosing St Bride's, 'the printers' church' in London, for the ceremony. They lived in splendour in the Chicago suburb of Highland Park in a house designed for them by their friend Frank Lloyd Wright. Cobden-Sanderson and others connected with the art of the book visited them there frequently, until 1914, when they moved to Pasadena.

In Southern California, George Millard dealt in books and art, finding treasures for the wealthy West Coast collectors and bibliophiles he cultivated, helped always by Alice, who was quickly invited to join a number of prominent cultural organizations, including the fashionable and influential Friday Morning Club. The club was an intellectual and cultural centre for women, which provided the Millards with many of their clients. George Millard often lectured there on books and collecting. When he died, on 6 November 1918 at seventy-two, Alice found herself alone, with a retarded daughter to support at a special school. Although George had left her their home and a modest inheritance, she had no choice but to earn money. The work she chose was to continue to pursue the rare-book trade, in which her husband, with her help, had made a satisfactory living for more than fifty years.

Catalogue No. 1 December, 1929

Old and Rare Books
Modern First Editions
Fine Illustrated Books
Books about Books
Etching, Engraving, Etc.

"How I pity all our Great Ones and Rich Men who know not this Happiness."
—Heinsius

Roy V. Sowers

Formerly of the Henry E. Huntington Library

Fine Prints - Rare Books

1005 East Green St.
Pasadena, California

Telephone, Wakefield 4827
Telegrams, Sowers, Pasadena

Alice Millard quickly put her mark on the collectors of the Los Angeles area and beyond, as an independent and knowledgeable connoisseur and businesswoman, who did not hold the rare-book brotherhood of the day in awe. She is thought to have been the first woman to bid openly at an auction at Sotheby's, where, at a sale in 1920, she defeated some of the leading dealers in the world to secure a manuscript of Froissart's *Chronicles*, which she sold immediately, and at a good profit, to the collector W.C. Van Antwerp. As well, using her friendships with Cobden-Sanderson, Sydney Cockerell and William Morris's widow, May, she managed to develop a near-monopoly in the United States on the works of the great designers, printers and binders of the English book renaissance. In 1923, she moved from Casa de las Floras, the pleasant but unprepossessing home she and George had lived in since settling in Pasadena, to a new house, again one designed by Wright. La Miniatura, as she called it, was situated on a wild and beautiful ravine which had been popularly thought to be unfit for building purposes. The house came to be considered among Wright's finest works. He himself certainly thought highly of it, for he mentions it frequently in his autobiography, and it was regularly photographed by architects, students, visitors and the curious. In later years, Millard added a small museum wing to the house, where she held exhibitions of books and art.

For the next fifteen years, combining scholarship, business acumen and judicious flattery, Alice Millard became *the* dealer in rare books and all things fine and desirable to the wealthy, but culturally uncertain, new rich of the Los Angeles area. In this, she was immeasurably blessed with exquisite good taste and with wonderful connections to the greatest rare-book dealers in Europe and the United States, such as Kenneth and Ernest Maggs, Bernard Quaritch, Seymour de Ricci and E.P. Goldschmidt, so that by her death (of cancer, in 1938) she had become one of the most influential booksellers in California, responsible for developing some of the finest libraries and collections on the West Coast.

When Sowers arrived in California he found Pasadena, with its millionaires' row stretching out along Orange Grove Avenue, to be a most desirable postal address. The Millards had chosen well in settling there thirteen years earlier, for Pasadena, which called itself the City of Roses, was already a community with a tradition of well-heeled artiness. Charles Fletcher Lummis and other late-nineteenth-century American artistic figures had built homes or studios there at the turn of the century; another long-time resident (a little incongruously) was Upton Sinclair, the socialist novelist. Pasadena was also home to the Stickney College of Art and to the influential theatre and drama school, the Pasadena Playhouse. Conservative, wealthy, but with what Sowers considered banal aesthetic tastes, Pasadena was a place in which he struggled vainly to feel at home. Describing his experiences with Alice Millard, Sowers admitted many years later to having been haughty and dismissive of Millard's *arriviste* clientele, for whom each visit to La Miniatura was stage-managed for maximum effect. 'I had to rearrange the furniture and wall hangings in order to set off some book we hoped to sell ... this technique never appealed to me personally, yet I have outlived my youthful naiveté and realise that such snob appeal has always been effective. The newly wealthy, I found, were so uncertain of themselves that the possession of recognised treasures helped establish their position.'

Robert Schad, who was the curator of the Huntington Library in 1938 when Alice Millard died, described a kind, generous and decent woman in the obituary he wrote in the Los Angeles *Times* the day after her death, noting that despite her wealth and the priceless nature of her stock, 'she never missed an opportunity to bring within the reach of a young or impecunious young collector an inexpensive item.' By contrast, Robert Rosenthal, in his essay 'Two Cities, Two Bibliophiles,' an appreciation of Alice Millard and Washington Irving Way, published in *A Bibliophile's Los Angeles* (1985), notes wryly that though Millard boasted of having cheaper books among her stock, 'She was never quite believed when she said that an inexpensive book could be acquired from her.' For his part, Sowers often did manage to put inexpensive but worthy books in the hands of poor collectors and cash-strapped librarians – perhaps a lesson he had learned from Alice Millard after all. Richard Press, a bookseller in Sacramento, remembers that when he was the librarian at Humboldt State University in Arcata in northern California in 1959, he bought a book from Sowers that 'was published in 1536 and contained early music printing. It was defective, lacking a few leaves, a trait of some of Roy's offerings which often provided impecunious collectors and libraries the opportunity to buy great books at a fraction of their market value.'

Without doubt, Sowers too must have benefited from Millard's generosity. Despite his youthful intellectual snobbery, working at La Miniatura gave him the opportunity to handle and appreciate books by the great English book artists from Blake to Morris as well as fine-press books such as those from Cobden-Sanderson's Doves Press. The experience also gave him the confidence to pass judgement on them. His employer also taught him much about bookselling as such. Late in 1927, however, his appointment at the Huntington Library was confirmed, and he went to work there for a year in the fields of modern first editions, fine illustrated books, prints and early maps, as an assistant to Millard's obituarist, Robert Schad, whom Henry Huntington had appointed as the curator of his own private rare-book collection at the end of the Great War. Schad served as the institution's curator until his death in 1963, a distinguished career of some forty-five years.

Sowers used the period at the Huntington as an opportunity to further his education as an antiquarian by making thousands of notes about the books he came across, to familiarise himself with the great works, writers, illustrators and printmakers of the past as well as with the talents of contemporary American fine printers such as John Henry Nash, Bruce Rogers, Daniel Berkeley Updike and the Grabhorn brothers, Edwin and Robert, who became his lifelong friends. Yet in his introduction to Catalogue Seventy-nine, the last one he issued, in 1969, Sowers ruefully acknowledges, 'During my apprenticeship at the Huntington Library, I wasted a lot of time copying second- and third-rate Elizabethan verse of a bawdy nature from the Bridgewater volumes and elsewhere; looking at these notes after a lapse of forty years, their destruction seems no loss.' Nonetheless it was during this period, too, that he developed his passion for fine prints, a field in which he traded with scholarly distinction for the rest of his life. Introducing a selection of prints he was offering for sale (including originals by Dürer, Breughel the Elder, Hollar and van Leyden) in Catalogue Fourteen in December 1934, he writes: 'I dreamed for years of being able to possess a Rembrandt etching; and, as I look back, it does not seem to me that it was any misfortune to me that I was able to buy at a low price a rather poorish impression of one of the commoner beggar subjects. I know that I derived tremendous mental satisfaction from this purchase, and that it spurred me to others.'

For reasons which, years later, he admitted he still found puzzling, Sowers left the security of his position at the Huntington in 1928, and started out on what was to be the course of the rest of his life, as a dealer in rare books, maps and prints. At the time he was living at an address on East Holly, which the 1928 city directory shows to have been the Pasadena YMCA. In November of that year, Sowers received news of the death in London, Ontario, of his brother, Herbert Earl, who died on the twentieth of the month; he was only thirty. Roy Vernon Sowers made one of his irregular trips back to Canada.

By the time the Pasadena city directory for 1929 was published, Sowers had moved into a new shop and print room at 117 North Marengo. In April 1929, the Print Makers Society of California, of which Sowers was a member, noted in its newsletter that it had held its second exhibition 'at Sowers' Gallery.' It was here, too, that Sowers announced an exhibition and sale of 'choice antiques – the private collection of Mr Ralph N. Earle.' But he could not have stayed at the North Marengo address for long, as he issued his very first catalogue as a bookseller eight months later, in December 1929, giving his address as 1005 East Green Street, Pasadena.

Sometime in 1929 Sowers must have married; the city directory for 1930, which would have been prepared in the second half of 1929, lists Roy Vernon Sowers and Pauline B. Sowers, Booksellers, at the

East Green Street store, with a home at 1217 Armada Drive (although they moved quite soon afterwards to an address on Maylin Avenue, where they lived until they left the city two years later). Pauline Bridge Seeberger, known to her friends as Polly, came from a wealthy and sophisticated family, and although she never completed either high school or university, she spoke excellent French and moved with aplomb in cultivated circles. Her father, Charles D. Seeberger, was a Chicago ironmonger who was involved in the invention and development of the escalator and had become wealthy by selling out to the Otis interests. He himself collected fine books and prints and gave many of both from his collection to the Huntington Library. A gift to his daughter of $200,000 enabled her husband to become a bookseller and develop both his expertise and his business without too much thought for financial difficulties, and in the 1930s they must have lived quite comfortably.

Sowers's first catalogue, which included rare books, modern first editions, fine prints, wood-engravings and etchings and decorative maps, ran to twenty-four pages and contained six hundred and eighty-seven items, including a leaf from a Gutenberg Bible and fourteen other assorted incunabula leaves, first editions of D.H. Lawrence, Christopher Morley, Carl Sandburg, Aldous Huxley and Somerset Maugham, and examples of fine press books from the Grabhorn, Vines, Nonesuch and Shakespeare Head presses, a Golden Cockerel edition of poems by Swift with wood-engravings by Robert Gibbings, and copies of the *Fleuron*, the influential English quarterly of typography and book history. As for his catalogue prices, which throughout his life he always claimed to be among the lowest in North America, his mint-condition copy of *The Waste Land*, published in New York in 1922, cost ten dollars; D.H. Lawrence's *Love Poems and Others* of 1913 was thirteen dollars; and his exceptionally fine and clean copy of Camden's *Britannia*, a large 1695 folio with an engraved portrait and fifty double-page maps, cost forty-eight. These entries, taken together with a footnote on the second page, in which Sowers promised that his second catalogue would contain a fourth folio Shakespeare dating from 1685, make it clear that he was already a clever and assiduous acquisitor, issuing a first catalogue that would have been the envy of many or most well-established book dealers. Styling himself on the catalogue cover as 'formerly of the Henry E. Huntington Library,' although he had spent barely a year there, he sought to represent himself as an old and experienced hand. He was just thirty-two. Towards the end of his career (in Catalogue Seventy-five, listing books from his private collection), he recalls 'a passion for the History of Printmaking and Book Illustration, dating from my days at the Huntington Library in 1928. Sometimes I wonder if I became a bookseller primarily as an excuse for collecting; certainly I did not find my enthusiasms widely shared by those frequenting my Pasadena and San Francisco bookshops in those far-off days. Today, preparing to relinquish books and prints treasured for a lifetime, I am a little surprised both at their significance and their diversity – English black letter printing, out of the way Book Illustration, even a number of Woodcut Books around 1500!' But such nostalgia was a long way in the future: in 1928, Sowers was a young bookseller with his career still to be established.

Several months elapsed before he published his second catalogue, in the summer of 1930. Book collectors today will marvel at the range of the more than six hundred modern first editions he listed, and grieve for a time when these were realistic prices – Eliot's *Ash Wednesday* and *For Lancelot Andrewes* at $1.75 and $3.25; a first English edition of Robert Frost's *Selected Poems* for $1.50 (although an uncut *North of Boston* of 1914 was in the catalogue at seventy-five); Aldous Huxley's *Crome Yellow* at six dollars; and sixteen Shaws, the least expensive of them a Fabian Society tract at only seventy-five cents. Given Sowers's distaste for the modern world, which he had developed early in life but which grew into almost a phobia through the 1930s, 1940s and 1950s, his promotion of such 'modern' writers is more than a little ironic: 'I think this Catalogue will appeal to a catholicity of tastes,' he wrote in his introductory notes, 'but my own interests and preferences run rather to the men of tomorrow than to unloading the 'highspots' of yesterday. I believe that a great many of the books listed here will have a future importance entirely disproportionate to their present price. This enthusiasm applies particularly to the work of such men as H.E. Bates, L.A.G. Strong, Maurice Hewlett, Robert Nathan, Henry Williamson, Humbert Wolfe, Roy Campbell, John Austen etc.' He went on: 'In fact, a discriminating collector might well buy whole sections of this catalogue en bloc. Consider the collection of low-priced items by John Drinkwater, and the new Poet Laureate (John Masefield).'

Sowers was a young man bursting with the vitality and confidence of the era when he issued Catalogues One and Two. Much can be learned by examining the other seventy-seven catalogues issued over a career of more than forty years. One sees how his interests changed, from contemporary books and creative writers almost exclusively in 1929 and 1930, to a final catalogue in 1969 that contained more than 325 books, not one of them a work of twentieth-century imaginative literature. As he commented in the introduction to that final catalogue, 'Of the world's literature through the centuries, what seems important varies from age to age – and with every individual; what we value today, may well be considered worthless tomorrow, just as one's enthusiasms at twenty have changed to others at seventy.'

One interest, however, remained almost constant over those four decades. Since the days of his Toronto print-room, the New Gallery, Sowers had been a knowledgeable scholar of prints in all media, and catalogued many, both the very rare and the more quotidian. As a number of invitations and newspaper clippings pasted in his scrapbook show, he also lectured to various groups about prints and the graphic arts. One invitation is for a subscription series of ten weekly lectures, which he gave at his print-room on East Green Street. The fee was ten dollars for the series, which covered German woodcuts, Dürer, French etchers, Van Dyke, the English school and Japanese prints. Around the same time, he opened a print gallery, the De La Guerra Studios, on Anacapa Street in Santa Barbara, where he held a summer exhibition of 'Colour Woodcuts' (he was still using Canadian spelling at this time but his orthography was never consistent –

and his punctuation never less than odd). No further mention of this gallery appears in Sowers's catalogues, papers or memorabilia.

Prints were such an important part of his life and work that in 1932 Sowers issued the *Collector*, the first of what was intended as an occasional listing of really fine engravings, etchings, woodcuts and maps. Prefaced with a scholarly and lucid 'Note on Early German Woodcuts,' the *Collector*, No. 1, lists works by Dürer, Jost Amman, Michael Wolgemuth and others, as well as fine sporting prints and some books. 'I cannot advertise a million books in stock,' Sowers wrote, 'but I have, what is more unusual, a selection of some 3,000 volumes which may be properly described as Real Books ...' No further issues of the *Collector* seem to have been issued, perhaps because he always found it more economical to sell prints through his regular catalogues.

The Sowers's first child, Anthony, had been born in Pasadena in May 1932; their second, a daughter, Lucia, would be born in San Francisco in 1936. In 1934, Sowers and Pauline were registered as the authors of a book entitled *Prints*, which was to be produced by the Esto Printing Company of Pasadena as part of a series entitled Enjoy Your Museum. Publishing it was their last public act in Pasadena.

‹ *San Francisco* ›

THE ENERVATING Southern California weather, together with what he perceived as the low level of intellectual life in the Pasadena area, persuaded Sowers that he needed to move somewhere more stimulating and congenial. Consequently, in 1934, he and Pauline moved to San Francisco, where Sowers rented a store at 451 Post Street, next to the St Francis Hotel, and sent out cards to his 'Clients and friends in the Trade' announcing that it was his intention to 'devote [his] efforts to even finer things than in the past …' The accommodations also housed his new print shop and exhibition space, Sowers's Print Rooms, at which he subsequently mounted regular exhibitions of drawings, prints, painting, sculpture and antique furnishings and fittings. Accompanying the handsomely printed invitations was a separate announcement that J.H. Allen, 'formerly a partner of Messrs. Vickery, Atkins and Torry [who] needs no introduction to San Francisco print collectors,' was to be his associate. The new shop featured walnut bookshelves bought from the famous Bohemian Club (its premises were being demolished at the time) and wonderful open-faced cases purchased from John Henry Nash (1871-1947), an important Californian fine printer who worked between 1916 and the mid-1930s, and whose books, superficially at least, owe a great deal to the design ideals of William Morris.

Nash was one of the first American fine printers of the twentieth century, and the printer of choice to the wealthy and well established. As a young man he had apprenticed in Toronto with one of the city's major jobbing and book printing firms, James Murray and Co, whose printing offices were on Front Street, just west of Yonge. Curiously, Nash saw a great deal of Canada as a professional cyclist who raced at venues throughout Ontario, Québec and on the Prairies, and when he was not racing, laboured in various cities and towns as a compositor, before returning to the United States to work in the printing trades, mostly in the San Francisco area. In 1916, he set up in business as an independent printer and publisher at last, with offices in San Francisco, where he displayed his own wonderful library of printing books and ephemera ranging from the fifteenth century to the nineteenth.

An exquisite printer, among the first in America to espouse the revival of fine printing that had been under way in England and Europe for two or three decades, Nash became a founder-member of the Book Club of California and printed many of its presentation publications; he did similar work for the Grolier Club and other such groups as well. Like his English antecedents, Nash had an evangelical attitude towards printing, seeing it as an art on a par with painting and sculpture. Certainly the ostentation and decoration of his books brought him wealthy patrons. William Randolph Hearst had Nash produce a memorial volume to commemorate the death of his mother, Phoebe Apperson Hearst, in 1928; Nash charged Hearst forty thousand dollars for an edition of one thousand copies. Hearst was so pleased with the work that, when his father died some five years later, he had Nash produce a memorial volume for him, too, in the same quantity and at the same price. Nash's greatest achievement was undoubtedly his three-volume edition of Dante, a translation by Melville Best Anderson of Stanford University, published in 1929, but later historians of the book, while according him his place as an important influence, tend to decry his work as flashy and insubstantial. In his excellent descriptive critique *The Printed Book in America*, Joseph Blumenthal sums up Nash in a sentence. Pointing out that the elephant folio was the characteristic Nash book, Blumenthal writes: 'He made monumental books for clients who confused pomp and ostentation with beauty.' Towards the end, in 1934, Nash took a position teaching book arts in Oregon. So it was that Sowers was able to acquire his handsome bookshelves, which he promptly filled with two van loads of books brought from Pasadena.

The first catalogue issued from Post Street – Number Twelve – came out in 1934. Already the eager young modern of the first and second catalogues was beginning to show signs of the distempered outlook that is so often a feature of his writing later. 'Right now,' he begins, 'I feel the necessity of getting a few things off my chest ...'. Topics included his increasing disgust that the educated classes in America were not buying books. 'For the moment, it is the fashionable thing to say that books are luxuries. But bathtubs and motorcars and cocktails are luxuries; and I find no statistical evidence of any serious mortality among the beauty-shops of this land of the fair.' Towards the end of the essay, in response to his own rhetorical musings about the excuses he imagined the American public offered for not buying books, he explodes, 'Depression be damned ... With the exception of the period of this brief, crazy [recession] of recent memory, there has never been a people better supplied with wealth than is America at present ... yet the paradoxical fact remains that the richest nation the world has ever known, 'cannot afford' the only things which will make its greatness equal its wealth!' The philistinism of the American public and its institutions and the betrayal of an intellectual heritage – these were themes he would revisit often.

Sowers published four catalogues while at the Post Street store, including Catalogue Fourteen, in December 1934, which offered twenty works from the Grabhorn Press, an accolade that demonstrates how important he thought Grabhorn titles were as examples of American fine press books. Edwin and Robert Grabhorn were born into a printing family in Indiana. As a young man in Seattle, Ed Grabhorn achieved a measure of fame as an expert music printer, but returned to Indianapolis in 1915, where he set up the Studio Press as a jobbing shop. Robert, younger by two years, joined him in 1917, and at Christmas 1919 they moved to San Francisco, and established the Grabhorn Press the following year. Until the press closed finally in 1965, they did a great deal of commissioned fine printing for private clients, including much for the Book Club of California. Their finest book was undoubtedly their large folio *Leaves of Grass* (1930), a copy of which, autographed by Edwin Grabhorn and annotated by him as

An Almanack for Booklovers

Comprising A BOOKMAN'S CALENDAR, also A CURIOUS ANTHOLOGIE selected from divers Authours these past 500 Yeares, and ADORNED WITH CUTS.

The Whole gathered together and Printed for ROY VERNON SOWERS, Booke-seller, at the Sign of the Reading Monk, Number 518 on Powell Street Hill, in the Citie of San Francisco, in the Yeare MCMXLII.

'the first trial binding by Hazel Dries,' Sowers would list several times. In Catalogue Fourteen, Sowers also notes approvingly the Grabhorns' publication of *The Printing Press*, 'a series of little brochures [which are] among the most sought-after Grabhorn 'incunables'.' Other remarkable Grabhorn productions in Sowers's catalogues were the *Philobiblon of Richard de Bury* with specially designed initial letters by Donald McKay, *A Printer's Paradise* by the great American typographer Theodore DeVinne, and the beautiful *The Santa Fe Trail to California*, a nineteenth-century travel journal by H.M.T. Powell with drawings by the author. A history and bibliography of the Grabhorn Press – in three volumes, for they did a very great deal of work – appeared between 1940 and 1973, while the press itself survived in a transmuted form, taken over by another fine Bay Area printer, Andrew Hoyem, who incorporated the Grabhorns' plant and extensive range of types into his Arion Press, using these assets to print many of his own fine books. Introducing the work of the Grabhorns in a catalogue note three months after having held an exhibition of their work at his Post Street gallery, Sowers writes: 'During the last two weeks of September, my entire mezzanine floor was devoted to a very comprehensive exhibition of the work of this Press. Some 200 items were on view, including books, broadsides and early specimen sheets, many of great rarity. The exhibition attracted a great deal of attention, and curiously enough, I am told it was the first such show ever held. It is impossible to view such an exhibition without marvelling at the versatility of these printers. To use one style of printing successfully is uncommon, and creditable; but the ability to work at will in the delicate tradition of Aldus or that of England's first printer; to one day emulate William Morris, and the next to rival the Doves Press – this is genius. Personally, I am confirmed in my opinion that the Grabhorns are America's greatest printers.' But even at the low prices he asked, Sowers had difficulty interesting collectors; the exhibition was not a financial success. Sowers turned to the Grabhorn brothers when he wanted to publish books of his own, using them for more than thirty years to print four books, including a bibliography of the influential Roxburghe Club, a society of San Francisco book lovers and collectors to which Sowers belonged most of his life.

Catalogue Fourteen also gives delightful evidence of Sowers's wide-ranging, squirrel-like attention to the arcane history and lore of his trade. Commenting on a first edition of *The Game and Playe of Chesse*, which Caxton printed at Bruges in 1475, before he began printing books in England, Sowers notes: 'This volume was picked up for twopence in the 18th Century, on a stall in a Dutch town, by a book-hunter named Wilson, better known as 'Snuffy Davy'. He sold it for £20 plus another £20 in books (the profiteering rascal!) to the London bookseller Osborne (the one knocked down by Dr Johnson with one of his own folios – 'Sir, he was impertinent to me.') who in turn sold it to Dr Askew for sixty guineas; and on his death it passed to the Royal Library at Windsor for £170. There is a perfect copy of the book in the King's Library of the British Museum, but Mr William Blades has shown that this is not 'Snuffy Davy's' copy, nor does the copy in the Henry E. Huntington Library correspond to Jonathan Oldbuck's description of the above copy. Later bibliographers declare that the book was not printed in England, but in Bruges, and Mr Blades says the whole 'Snuffy Davy' story is apocryphal.' Sowers does not join in the argument, but the entry lacks a price nonetheless, a fact explained by his conclusion: 'Every book catalogue should include at least one item which is not for sale, if only as a reminder to certain collectors that some things cannot be translated into dollars and cents. For my part, I can only say that no conceivable sum of money will ever induce me to part with this little volume.'

A man of decided and prejudiced (about books) opinions, Sowers dotted Catalogue Fourteen with quotations that give a clear idea of what he felt the importance of good books to be. 'Books must be expensive,' he quotes at one point from V.V. Rozanov's *Fallen Leaves*. 'Books aren't vodka. A book must be proud, free and independent. On this account it must above all be expensive.' Yet Sowers frequently notes that he will not sell his books for the maximum the market will bear but rather at prices fair to genuine collectors, returning to him only enough profit to make the transaction worthwhile. Indeed, many of Sowers's catalogue introductions over the years were preoccupied with money – how much he could buy and sell books for, how much he lost when his pear harvest failed, how iniquitous American taxation and fiscal policy were. In Catalogue Fourteen, he writes: 'I have been trying to think how long it is since anyone has looked at a fine Print or fine Book of mine and said, "How fine!" rather than "How much?"' And he inveighs against collectors who become so obsessed with the idea of getting a bargain that they forget there is such a thing as quality. 'They may be collectors, or they may be coster-mongers; connoisseurs they are not.'

The Post Street print-room was enlarged and redecorated in 1935, and a well-known San Francisco artist, Sybil Olive Martin, was hired to supervise the decorative print and framing departments. Although it had not sold well, Sowers's Grabhorn show had been well reviewed in the San Francisco newspapers and Sowers persisted in his belief that fine printing was worth exhibiting. A few months later, on 3 August 1935, he opened another exhibition, 'Fine Books and Printing,' this one from the presses of Johnck and Seeger and the Windsor Press and followed it with exhibitions of printing by John Henry Nash at the end of that month and yet another Grabhorn one in September. Nothing exists to let us know whether these were more successful than the original Grabhorn exhibition, but one suspects the worst, since if he had a hit, Sowers would have boasted of it in one of his essays.

Catalogue Fifteen, issued in December 1935, was the last from the Post Street address. Shortly afterwards, Sowers moved to 117 Montgomery Street, where he issued his next catalogue, in April 1936, the month his daughter, Lucia, was born. The Catalogue Fifteen essay became something of a favourite of booksellers, confronting and scorning, as it does, the buying habits of university and public libraries and their parsimonious support for local (that is, American and especially Californian) book-makers and dealers. Sowers prefaces his remarks by quoting Dr Johnson's weary reply to the Earl of Chesterfield's famously opportunistic (and belated) offer of help in publishing his new dictionary: 'Is not a patron, my Lord, one who looks with unconcern on a man struggling for life in the water, and when he has reached the ground, encumbers him with help?' Sowers's argument is that the great American institutional libraries, while paying lip service to the notion of supporting indigenous rare book dealers and publishers of fine books, were buying from European sources, ignoring American suppliers. He condemns their librarians for practising intellectual snobbery, and notes the number of American dealers who had gone bankrupt, in contrast to a number of dealers in Europe who could boast of living entirely off the profits of selling to one or two American academic institutions. 'I know all the answers customarily given by the Libraries and Museums: funds are limited; our appropriations are cut; we can buy more cheaply abroad; we must economise!' he writes. 'I maintain that it is highly doubtful that you *do* save, but supposing you do, what then? Does a Museum exist in a vacuum? Is a University founded at great cost for the purpose of stifling local cultural development, that it may, temporarily, save a little on its book purchases?' He concludes, with typical verve: 'One of the few reasons that I should like to inherit a million dollars is that I should like to try to prove that even one great Print and Book Shop is probably a damned sight more important to a community than many of the costly institutions on which we spend our money! Now I feel better, and I wish you all a very Merry Christmas – with increased appropriations.'

The first book that Sowers engaged the Grabhorns to print for him was announced on the inside cover of Catalogue Sixteen, dated April 1936. *The Two Editions of Dante's Divine Comedy, Venice 1491* was to have been Sowers's own essay on a famous series of woodcuts. The two 1491 editions of Dante to which the title refers appeared in March and November of that year, respectively, and are essentially identical except that in the latter version one block is recut. Sowers wrote: 'My enthusiasm for the Woodcuts of the Fifteenth Century is now of some five years' duration ... and when, about a year ago, I was able to acquire an incomplete copy of the

Dante of March 1491, I resolved to issue a monograph for the benefit of those who might share this enthusiasm.' The book was to have been published in October 1936 or possibly earlier, in an edition limited to ninety copies selling at twenty-five dollars each, with three copies printed on vellum, specially bound, each containing an original leaf with a full-page woodcut, at fifty dollars. Sowers mooted as well a further two hundred copies, depending on demand, which we might call the trade edition, to be sold at fifteen dollars. But the project seems to have died from lack of interest. In subsequent catalogues, there is no further mention of an advance subscription. Neither is it mentioned in the Grabhorn Press bibliography. No doubt Sowers greatly overestimated the market.

As with most of Sowers's lists, Catalogue Sixteen is full of interesting arcana. Of Henry Neville's *Island of Pines*, an imaginary and highly wrought narrative of travel and adventure, published in London in 1668, he notes: 'The history of the pamphlet is the subject of an interesting book, *The Isle of Pines* by Worthington Chauncey Ford, published by the Club of Odd Volumes, Boston, 1920. The details of the narrative are necessarily of a somewhat coarse and indecent character.' Of a copy of Drayton's *Poly-Olbion* of 1622, Sowers observes that one of the maps 'shows an international Eisteddfod in progress, with English and Welsh choirs competing across the Severn …' The *Poly-Olbion*, he suggests, was 'the sort of book that should never be sold. It is too interesting.' Nonetheless he lists it, fine and rare, at eighty dollars.

Sowers and his wife visited Europe in May 1936, and Catalogue Seventeen, sent out in December of that year, the same month he gave a talk on the European book scene to the Roxburghe Club, offers an interesting view of the rare-book world as it stood on the brink of the second great war of the century: 'Since issuing my last Catalogue, I have been Bookhunting in Spain, which I left some two weeks before the outbreak of the present War [that is, the civil war in Spain, which began in July 1936]; in Paris; in England and Scotland; and in the Eastern United States … I attended virtually every sale of consequence during last summer in London; I talked to scores of dealers and collectors; I think that I handled personally at least a million books; and I bought plenty ... I observed great changes in the booktrade ... that fine Old Books are rare, and that the market for them is a rising one. There is no longer any depression among the London booksellers, and again they are paying record prices in the auction rooms. Already, too, the larger English dealers are quietly but steadily buying important books back from America ... At the moment, my mind, and my offices are in rather similar condition – one a jumble of impressions of two worlds – the other a jumble of packing cases and Books and Prints from at least two continents ...'

The material he then offers include Aiken's famous 1834 series of prints of the Quorn Hunt; a group of books illustrated by Arthur Rackham; a collection of Thomas Bird Mosher first editions; and a variety of books, prints and maps from Europe. His note on item 166, Elinor Glyn's *Three Weeks*, published in London in 1907, is characteristic of his erudition and humour. Glyn, who spent her first ten years in the agricultural town of Guelph, Ontario, before moving to Europe with her mother and stepfather, became to popular literature, the stage and films in the first decades of the century what Danielle Steele perhaps is to our own times. She was lauded and lionized in London and Hollywood and was the adored mistress of Lord Curzon, the former viceroy of India. But today her claim to immortality all rests on her coining the concept of *It*, to describe the vibrant sensuality of the actress Clara Bow, and for writing a scene in *Three Weeks* in which a romantic interlude takes places on a tiger-skin rug. The second accomplishment led one poetaster to write: 'Would you like to sin / With Elinor Glyn / On a tiger skin? / No, I'd prefer / To err with her / On some other fur.' Sowers offered *Three Weeks* for ten dollars with the note, '*Three Weeks*! How many girls have been expelled from boarding school for illicit possession of this purple classic! During twenty-odd years, what heights of wickedness it represented! ... For the first time, I have glanced through this hectic romance – which is said to be based on truth – but I cannot recommend it for reading purposes. Here is a specimen: 'And the loveliest sight of all, in front of the fire, stretched at full length ... reclined the lady, garbed in some strange clinging garment of heavy black purple crepe, its hem embroidered with gold ... her back supported by a pile of velvet cushions, and a heap of rarely bound books at her side, while between her red lips was ...' I hate to think how many millions have been sold, but this is a First Edition, and the damned thing is rare!'

Despite the undoubted intellectual stimulation of San Francisco, Sowers was not happy there, and, at some time in 1937, as he was to write in an essay 'Bookselling in the Mountains,' he and Pauline bought 'a small ranch in the Santa Cruz mountains and began the long process of making it habitable ...' They moved in as soon as possible but did not relocate the inventory of books and prints until 'shortly after Pearl Harbour ...' Meanwhile, they collaborated on an edition of *Joan of Orleans*, announced in the introduction to Catalogue Twenty and published in the spring of 1938. This was a version of the Jeanne d'Arc story taken from the *Chronicles of St Denis* in the *Chroniques de France* (Paris, 1493), translated by Pauline and edited by her husband, with reproductions of woodcuts from the original edition; the Grabhorn brothers printed it. 'The *Chroniques de France*,' he wrote in the beautifully printed flier for the book, 'were the official annals of the kingdom, compiled by the monks of the abbey of St. Denis, from 1122 to the end of the reign of Charles VII in 1461, and it is from the final portion of these Chronicles, written by Jean Chartier, that this most contemporary account of Jeanne d'Arc is taken. The translation is made from the beautiful edition printed in Paris in 1493 by Antoine Vérard.' When he offered the book in a catalogue for the first time, he wrote: 'It was my aim to make this book one of the outstanding examples of modern fine book-making, and I have been much gratified by its reception. The great Museums and Libraries – from the Metropolitan in New York to the Huntington in Pasadena – , Private Collectors, east and west, Booksellers, especially, and unexpectedly, those in the east, are sending a daily rising flood of orders and repeat orders.' Certainly the book justifies his claim for it as a fine example of the craft: a folio of thirty-six pages in double columns, set entirely by hand in Rudolf Koch's imposing

YOU are cordially invited to attend an exhibition of books, pamphlets, broadsides, etc., printed by the Grabhorn Press. The exhibition will include many specimens, now rather scarce, of the early work of this press, an interesting group of experimental pages, as well as its more elaborate productions. Open from 10 to 6 until the sixth day of October.

ROY VERNON SOWERS
451 Post St., San Francisco

Bible Gothic type, with chapter headings in red and initials in red and blue, and twenty woodcuts by Antoine Vérard from the original edition and a bibliographical note by Sowers. The book is bound in the Kelmscott style, with the coat of arms of Jeanne d'Arc wood-blocked in gold and colours on the front. The paper is a heavy Leonardo, fifteen by ten and one-half inches, and the edition limited to five hundred and twenty-five copies. All for a modest price of six dollars, 'which is less than half what one normally expects to pay for such a book.'

In the same introduction, he announces his intention to publish his second fine book (or third, if we include his unrealized Dante project), 'a hitherto unpublished Manuscript of Sir Isaac Newton on Alchemy.'

The book was to have had an introduction by Dr Louis T. More of the University of Cincinnati, a noted authority on alchemy and the author of a Newton biography published in 1934. The proposed work was to be printed by the Grabhorns in an edition of eighty copies, each containing a sheet from the original manuscript 'in Sir Isaac Newton's hand.' Sowers may have picked up the manuscript on his European travels the previous year and decided he would make more by parsing it out this way than by selling it whole. Whatever the impetus to publish, the Newton book, like the Dante, never appeared and was never mentioned in his lists again.

Catalogue Twenty concludes, as so many of his later catalogues do, with a lyrical reflection on the ranch, to which he and his family seem to have gone only to spend the summers at this point. 'By the time this second book is printed,' he writes, 'I fancy it will again be time to seek 'country contentments'. The deer have had almost undisturbed possession of my Santa Cruz ranch for some months now; they don't help the fruit trees, but they can't harm the view.'

Each year, Sowers put together a Christmas catalogue, offering books, prints and cards for the yuletide trade. Catalogue Twenty-three (misnumbered as Thirty-three), in 1939, was one such, with a specially printed Christmas cover and the entries interspersed with seasonal quotations: a pretty little production, containing the usual

Sowers musings, such as when he considers the attractions of fine prints. He describes an evening spent looking at prints by Dürer, Blake and Samuel Palmer, works he calls 'the inheritance and the justification of Collecting. A line in Horace, – a leaf of old Printing, – an Engraving by Dürer, – and suddenly the doors of the centuries are opened for communion with the greatest minds of another Age.' He then goes on to shill for specific books in the catalogue, beautiful but, by implication, lacking usefulness. But so what? 'We are told that the *first* Christmas gifts included *frankincense* and *myrrh*, than which, less useful presents can scarcely be imagined. Perhaps we need, now and then, to remind ourselves that their lack of usefulness was of their very essence.'

Later in the catalogue, he returns to his edition of Jeanne d'Arc, by this time advertised as *Joan, the Maid of Orleans*. It is, he says, 'his serious attempt to produce a volume of authentic Mediaeval flavour, and above all, to produce it worthily. I believe this has been accomplished ... the volume as a whole is a happy example of the finest work of the Grabhorn Press.' In contrast to his earlier claims concerning the many 'great Museums and Libraries' which had bought it, he now states that there are 'but three copies in America, my own, and those in the N.Y. Public Library and the Newberry Library [of Chicago] respectively.' Perhaps the Huntington had already disposed of its copy.

In 1939 and 1940 he brought out two interesting linked catalogues, numbers Twenty-four and Twenty-five. Sowers called them his *Biblio-Gallimaufry* and *Biblio-Gallimaufry II*. The first contained 'A Hotch-Potch, Olla Podrida, or Hasty Pudding for the Delectation and Diversion of All Booklovers, Poetasters, Snatch-Wits, Persevering Pedants, Random readers, Dabblers in Heliconian Springs – ' while the second is wrapped in a complicated and jumbled typographical cover, which Sowers labels 'Portrait of a Bookseller's mind during the preparation of a general Catalogue.' An unusual feature of Twenty-four is that Sowers offers 'books in bundles,' a fact he billboards on the cover with the line, 'A discourse on Bundling (Not what you think!)' He lists twenty-eight bundles of books made up from fifty crates he had recently bought but had no room for. They focused on American fine printing, first editions, publications of the Navarre Society or books about electricity, and ranged from two dollars and fifty cents to twelve dollars a lot. Sowers writes that 'while I have great affection for many a friendly volume which I have loved long since, it's a case of 'How happy could I be with either, were t'other dear charmer away!'' He concludes that the bundles are offered at a fraction of his costs and thus on a purely cash basis – cheque with order. What book-lover receiving the catalogue could have passed up, at $8.50, an 'American Fine Printing' bundle containing works by the great American typographers Bruce Rogers and D.B. Updike and examples of products of the Harbour, Merrymount, Riverside and Lakeside presses, as well as books by Mosher and Nash?

Biblio-Gallimaufry II was the result of the favourable response enjoyed by its predecessor, which by its variety and catholicity had brought in many new customers. Sowers assured his clients that the catalogue 'includes many book bargains, [as] any reader may readily see for himself.' Never one to pass up an opportunity to allow others to benefit from his own opinions, Sowers takes time to deplore the trend of 'catalogues arranged strictly by author.' This idea, he contends, 'seems to me a regrettable modern innovation. It is less than 700 years since John Balbus, author of the encyclopaedic 'Catholicon', in adopting the alphabetical arrangement, felt obliged to devote considerable space to an explanation of the new system. After all, what is time to a Librarian, or a Bookseller? Many incorrigible book buyers are more interested in knowing what a book is about, than in the author's name; and to me it is unthinkable that Booksellers should permit deletion from their Catalogues of such well-worn words as Alchemy, Binding, Cookery, Juvenile, and Strawberry Hill, without protesting this invasion of ancient privilege!' Protesting that ancient privilege himself, he lists Cookery and California, Horses and Hydraulics, Scotland and Shakespeare – in the last-named instance, a fine copy of the 1756 Foulis Press collected works, as gathered and corrected by Alexander Pope. Under *Canada* he offers a copy of Susanna Moodie's *Roughing It in the Bush*, in the 1913 Foulis edition with coloured illustrations by R.A. Stewart, price $4.50. Under *Grabhorn Press* he has his own *Joan, the Maid of Orleans* at six dollars (the 'trade' edition) and notes that the sumptuously produced special collectors' version has just won Honourable Mention in a Rounce and Coffin Club exhibition of western books. Almost immediately on issuing the second *Gallimaufry*, Sowers sent off a four-page Thanksgiving Book Sale list, which, with twenty-nine entries, is just a taster for a house-clearing sale of more than four thousand volumes at his Montgomery Street shop – 'not just ordinary books, but real books, important books, scholarly books, and not a few that are damned rare!' How altogether characteristic of Sowers that even so brief a list should nevertheless contain so many enviable volumes: Dibdin's famous *Bibliotheca Spenseriana*; John Gerard's *Herball, or Generall Historie of Plantes*, on which Culpepper and later herbalists based their own works; *The Golden Legend* of Caxton, in the Kelmscott Press edition, with initial letters cut in wood by Edward Burne-Jones – as well as forty-seven volumes of *Punch*, 1893 to 1916. Sowers's 1602 copy of the Breeches Bible (Genesis 11:7 – 'and they sewed figge tree leaves together and made themselves breeches') reminds me of the one I found myself in a box of dusty old books at a country auction in rural England. It had been badly cut at the fore-edge, but contained dense annotations in every available margin, written in a crabbed hand by whomever had owned it in the late eighteenth century; I was excited to find it then, and I think I would be excited to find another today.

Sowers's father died 26 September 1940. His obituary in the London *Free Press* describes him 'father of Roy, of San Francisco, California …' This suggests that, despite having bought his run-down fruit farm, Sowers was still effectively living and working in the city, though the exact chronology of the move is difficult to determine; even Sowers's second wife, Margaret Cosgrave Sowers, can put the date only approximately, at around 1942. In any event, his catalogues continued to carry addresses in San Francisco. Moving from Montgomery Street in 1941, he issued Catalogues Twenty-seven and

Twenty-eight from 518 Powell Street. It was there, in late 1941 or early 1942, that he issued a list of forty-nine books entitled 'Closing Shop April 11th – Final Clearance of Books and Prints.' Thereafter his catalogues bear the address of the village of Glenwood, within whose boundaries the fruit farm, Topside, lay.

A book that crops up frequently in reference to Sowers is one he published privately in 1942, a seventy-six-page work he called *An Almanack for Booklovers*, a compilation of quotations about books and reading, 'the whole gathered together and printed for Roy Vernon Sowers, booke-seller at the Sign of the Reading Monk, Number 518 on Powell Street Hill, in the Citie of San Francisco, in the Yeare NCMXLII.'

This handsome little volume, now found in special-collections libraries with a serious interest in Californiana, is typical of the kind of thing private presses do so well. It also serves as a window onto the breadth of Sowers's reading and book-knowledge, for he quotes Milton on censorship, Leopardi's dialogue between a bookseller and a passerby, John Aubrey on Sir Thomas More and Ben Jonson, the little-known *Medicine to Winne Women*, Villega's *How to Be a Famous Physician*, Augustine Birrell's *Gossip in a Library* and an anonymous seventeenth-century squib, *The True Tale of the Tree Goose*. Characteristically, he makes an ironic little joke in the illustration he chose for the title-page, which was Brandt's 'Ship of Fools.'

Thus, in 1942, he seems finally to have closed his city bookshop and moved his stock to the farm, as he would explain later in Catalogue Thirty. The last two catalogues sent from San Francisco, numbers Twenty-seven and Twenty-eight, were, respectively, one of Americana/Californiana and a general list of old and rare books, although each has, in the modern expression, added value. Issuing a catalogue of Americana gave Sowers the opportunity, as the US entered the war, to reflect on weighty matters in the longest introductory essay he ever allowed himself. 'It is customary,' he writes, 'that my Catalogues carry something of personal comment, but grave times require grave words. 'The price of freedom is eternal vigilance' – and each of us needs to remember that our individual work or business or profession is wholly dependent on a certain way of life. Because we have been, all of us, too busy to be vigilant, we suddenly realize that our whole way of life is endangered. Therefore, I speak, not as a Bookseller, but as an American citizen.'

There follows an impassioned piece that ranges over America's obligations to Britain, the concept of Culture, a rebuttal of American isolationism and a swingeing attack on organized labour. If necessary steps are not taken, he argues, 'We shall see the American standard of living destroyed, and the status of American labour degraded beneath anything known in this century. And historians, looking back on the event, will marvel at our stupidity, and will draw the parallel of the Roman Emperor who fiddled while Rome burned.'

‹ *Los Gatos* ›

SOWERS BOUGHT HIS FRUIT FARM in the Santa Cruz hills about 1934, using six thousand dollars given to his wife by her mother, Emma Bridge Seeberger. At first they used it as a summer retreat, and built a house there in 1938. The following year, however, Roy and Pauline separated, divorcing in 1940. She returned to Pasadena, to live in her late mother's house with the two children; she later married Eric Gibberd, the director of the West Coast Community Chest in 1945 or 1946, and died in the summer of 1996.

Sowers stayed on in the city until 1942 before making Mountain Charley Road his permanent address. For a while, in fact, his catalogues give his postal address as Glenwood. Sometimes, however, *Glenwood* is overprinted with *Los Gatos*, while alumnus reference cards he returned to the University of Toronto at this time show him living at RR 1, Alma, California. No doubt the addresses all refer to his place in the hills above Los Gatos, in Santa Clara County.

Los Gatos was formalized as a town in 1850, taking a name that had been in use in the area much earlier, a reference to the wild cats that were prevalent in the hills. At one time, Los Gatos had been an important lumber centre, although by the time Sowers transplanted himself there the industry had dwindled and the town was known as much as anything for being the place where, in 1918, Father William E. Riker established a utopian community called Holy City, which survived until the 1950s.

Jasper Schad, son of Robert O. Schad, Sowers's first mentor at the Huntington Library in 1927, recalled, in a telephone interview with me in the autumn of 1996, his first meeting with Sowers during a family visit to Topside in the summer of 1939. 'My whole family went up from Pasadena to the [World's] Fair in San Francisco in

1939,' he recalled, 'and we stopped off and visited them at the farm. It was very, very primitive. I remember that they had only outhouses at that time. We didn't spend very long there, but Tony was there and I remember we played together, before we went up to the Fair.' Schad's recollection is that Sowers called the place Topside (although Sowers refers to it as Parnassus in a few catalogues). At any rate, the improbably-numbered 25000 Mountain Charley Road, Los Gatos, is the address that appears on all Sowers's catalogues from Twenty-eight onward.

Schad continued: 'The next time I saw Roy was in 1944, I think, by which time he was divorced from Polly, but not yet remarried. The children spent the summers with Roy at that time, and the rest of the time with their mother. She had bought a rather large Mediterranean place down in Pasadena. I remember distinctly their buying a 1940 Hudson Convertible, so their marriage had to have broken up very soon after we saw them that time in 1939. At any rate, in order to have someone to play with Tony, Roy invited me up for about a month, in 1944. This is where my memories of Roy are very good, and the reason for that is that it was a life so totally and utterly different from anything I'd ever known, that it is clearly fixed in my mind. Here was this man, living a very, very isolated life; there seemed to be few people around, and the people who *were* around were rural people, basically dust-bowl refugees. He had nobody working on the farm with him; he did it all himself, the little that got done. The orchards were somewhat decayed. I remember he had prunes, a lot of pears and a few apricots, and he didn't have anybody to help him. I suppose that was one of the reasons I went up there, because Tony and I were picking the fruit that month. He had a little pick-up truck, and once a week we'd go in to Santa Cruz to the grocery store to pick up supplies. We didn't seem to do anything else. We never seemed to have any contact with other people. There was a mail train that came through, and they tossed the bags on and off, and Tony and I would go down to the village [Glenwood] and watch them every day, around eleven o'clock in the morning.'

Sowers's son, Tony, fleshed out Schad's impressions in a letter to me. He wrote: 'The ranch was a back-to-the-land adventure similar to that engaged in by every generation. It suited Dad fine, but did not suit my mother well – she wanted more civilization and comfort! ... There was a very rudimentary house on [the land] when they bought it. It had an outhouse and running water from a redwood tank perched up the hill, below a seep. They lived in it, I believe, about a year, then moved to an original homestead cabin of similar construction but on top of the hill, near the home site ... They had to haul water in five-gallon milk pails, and I remember the dipper routine. Outhouse, wood cookstove, chickens, and a pony for me and Lucia. Dad had a team of horses and worked at restoring the orchard ... Dad was a strict disciplinarian [but] Mom was more sympathetic. The house they built was a major undertaking. Designed by my mother, [the house] had twenty-one doors (a sore point with Dad), a sleeping porch, two baths, and four rooms plus a loft office, a big living room, dining room and kitchen. They pumped water from the seep, a distance of three-quarters of a mile or more, to a twenty-thousand-gallon concrete tank on a hill above the house. I remember helping to lay, finally, the long-stored three-quarter-inch oak floors to get them down before Margaret moved in [about 1945.] I will not claim an idyllic childhood, but my parents were good people and did the best they could with what they had.'

Many years after these events, in the essay in Catalogue Seventy-six, Sowers expressed regret at the change and deterioration of the mountains since he first moved to Mountain Charley Road. He recalled 'the old village of Glenwood, 500 feet below, with its general store and post office, the narrow, twisty highway and the two or three daily trains running in and out of the tunnel through these hills. Beyond the little red schoolhouse where my son [this is the only mention of either of his children in six dozen such essays] learned his ABCs; beyond the decaying Glenwood Hotel where San Franciscans of another era were content to come by train for a quiet vacation in redwood country; the wooded hills & fields & pastures rose, ridge after ridge, past the knoll reputedly an ancient Indian burial ground, past a couple of dilapidated summer cabins almost

Joan, the maid of Orleans

Being that portion of the Chronicles of St. Denis which deals with her Life and Times. From the Chroniques de France, printed in Paris, 1493. Translated by Pauline S. Sowers. With reproductions of some twenty woodcuts from the original edition and a Bibliographical Note on the work of Antoine Verard.

Printed at the GRABHORN PRESS
for ROY VERNON SOWERS

hidden in the trees, past the distant geometric pattern of orchards on Vineland to the 3800 ft. flat top of Loma Prieta, with vineyards clinging to its flank ...'

The scornful Sowers of later life, so bitterly resentful at the commercialization of everything he held dear, and also at the hunger of his fellow Americans for meretricious acquisitions and spurious progress, was already in formation when Schad visited. In our interview, Schad recalled: 'Roy was, to me, very stern and kind of a hard person. Every time we'd do anything for him, he was always ... well, we'd earn money picking fruit, but he'd always find things we didn't do right, and he'd dock our pay. I remember him going over the accounts with us to work out what we were owed for our work, and then he would deduct my board and keep. I think it was all cleverly arranged so that I got less than ten dollars for the whole month's work! I definitely felt short-changed, but it was a summer like no other, and I shall always remember it. On balance, it was a good time.' Schad went on: 'Roy Sowers did seem a very hard and intense man. I know that about this time he was about to get married [to Margaret Cosgrave, the daughter of a California judge, in 1944], although we never did see Margaret while I was there. We never saw her, and I don't remember that he used to go anywhere, so they must have met some other way at that time.' And he recalled his final meeting with Sowers: 'I guess the last time I saw him was in 1951. Tony was up there at the ranch and I had bought another car, an old Chevrolet, and it needed some engine work, and they said to come on up and we would all work on it. And so I went up there and spent about a week or so. By that time he was married ... I'd grown up in a fairly conservative family; we just didn't know people like this! It was such a surprise and a shock to me to hear this kind of radical, political conversation, so it stuck in my mind. But I wouldn't say he was a real happy person. We'd go into town to shop, and everything we ate was out of cans. You know, Chef Boyardee ravioli out of cans, that kind of thing. And having grown up in a family where cooking and food were really something important, it was truly difficult for me, physiologically, to have to endure food like that. It was all such an unusual experience, which is why I remember it. He really made his business, in this period, travelling to England and buying up just about everything from the eighteenth century – when Europe was on the ropes. There was good money in that. But I'm amazed you say he left money to the Bodleian Library in Oxford, because you would never have thought it possible, he lived so frugally. During the war, everything was scarce, but even so, his car tires were worn down to the canvas, and he was always worrying about whether they would blow out. It must have been a very crabbed life.'

As for the farm itself, the setting made it 'a lovely place. The house was situated on a little knoll which is why, I suppose, they called it Topside. The orchards fanned out, and there was a road which separated the property, but on the backside there was a lovely little glen with redwoods and hazelnut trees. You'd go down and you could pick the nuts. It was just a charming, charming place. You could see forever, and I remember once looking off at a forest fire which must have been very many miles away.'

In a poetic essay in Catalogue Fifty, Sowers was to put a much different gloss on his life at the farm, although he frequently complained of how hard and ill-rewarding it was being a fruit farmer and a bookseller. Just as frequent a cause of complaint, of course, was his view that the twentieth century, with its various political, sociological and technological barbarities, was encroaching on him.

His first full catalogue from Topside – and the first one he illustrated with a photograph (in this case, of the view over the hills from the house) was Thirty, 'A Bookseller's Miscellany' of Americana, modern firsts, illustrated books, art, travel and literature: virtually the full range of Sowers's long-held professional interests. It was published in 1944 and is one of the last of his catalogues to list modern first editions in any appreciable number, for his attention seems to have been directed increasingly to the more arcane areas of the trade, particularly towards the history of science and medicine and herbals and other *materia practica*. Sowers does not mention any changes to his personal life in his catalogue introductions of the period. At first on his own, after the divorce from Polly, and latterly married to Margaret, he remained at Topside throughout the Second World War, selling books when he could and increasing fruit production in response to the federal government's appeal. In Catalogue Thirty, he wrote that he had felt a keen urge to contribute to the war effort despite his age (mid-forties). 'When I closed my San Francisco book shop, early in 1942, it was in the expectation of finding work I could do, either in uniform or directly connected with the War,' he wrote. 'This being a young man's war, that hope was disappointed. Meantime, it developed that food was a rather important item in the national economy; and having this ranch – with no one to operate it for me – I turned farmer.' He went on: 'It has been an interesting experience, and, incidentally, much more of a full-time job than I expected. The yearly round of essential tasks – pruning, spraying, cultivation and harvest – leaves less leisure for catalogues and bookish pursuits than I had hoped; but I remain a Bookseller and Print Dealer, temporarily within limitation. There have been times when I thought my new life approximated that of a cabbage; and at other times this life has seemed to have much more meaning than the usual round of city activities. One thing I have definitely learned: a very thorough respect for the American farmer.'

The undoubted centrepiece of the catalogue is a section of forty lots of Grabhorn Press books and ephemera spanning the period 1915 to 1940. The list begins with the Grabhorn bibliography by Elinor Raas Heller and David Magee, which enjoyed an introduction by Frederic Goudy himself, whose types the Grabhorn brothers had long favoured. Sowers's list includes a set of sixteen double-leaf trial proofs, set in a variety of different typefaces, of the press's indisputably great work, Whitman's *Leaves of Grass*, published in 1930. Also listed is Sowers's *Joan*, of course, about which he notes, 'The price on this book ($7.50) is ridiculously low. If produced today, it would be $15; and some advance in price on the few remaining copies may become necessary in the near future.' Six catalogues later he was still offering it at seven-fifty, although with the note, 'I don't know why I continue to sell my few remaining copies of this very fine book at this absurdly low price.' He would last list it in Catalogue Seventy-one, in 1962 or early 1963, by which time it really was marked at fifteen dollars.

Having established the pattern of mixing book information with reflections about farming, Sowers found that some customers would inquire after his experiences in the country and about rural life generally. 'For the benefit of the many who have expressed interest in my ranching activities,' he wrote in Catalogue Thirty-one, 'I may say that in these parts we received this year the highest price on record for Bartlett pears – almost one quarter that at which they sold in the retail stores; also, that, due to the vagaries of the weather, our crop was about 15 per cent of normal! For similar reasons, the apples sun-burned, and the prunes cracked on the trees. Poison oak was, as usual, a very successful crop, and if only Mr Henry Ford – or a paternal government – can discover a use for it, all of us hill-billies will be prosperous.' He added: 'The deer took to the woods during the hunting season, but now they are back again, feeding off my orchard and garden every night – and some days. They have come to regard me with mild tolerance, but occasionally – as when they chewed up my rose bushes – I am conscious of the disadvantages of being a law-abiding citizen. The gophers and jack-rabbits are plentiful, and the pack-rats still make nests under the hood of my little-used car. All of which is normal, and – perhaps on that account – refreshing, in these abnormal times. Also the sun rises every morning.'

At about this same time, in September 1945, Emma F. Sowers died at Victoria Hospital in London, Ontario. The London *Free Press* called her the 'dear mother of Roy V., of Alma, California ...'

‹ The Curmudgeon ›

SOWER'S DISTASTE FOR THE CENTURY in which he lived went forward apace. In Catalogue Thirty-two, his first one following the war, he addresses the question of America's pell-mell pursuit of novelty and consumerism, a trend that continued to provoke his disgust. 'Big business prospers by creating wants, – as distinct from needs, – and with the enthusiastic co-operation of the boys in advertising, the public is now being 'educated' to a whole new set of these wants (incidentally at a cost of billions of dollars in evaded taxes which could be used to reduce our war debt!).'

Getting and spending, he frets, will consume everyone's time and energy, and the book trades will be unable to compete – for novelty or excitement – with the new gadgets and gee-gaws in the homes of America. 'Henry Miller's title, 'The Air-Conditioned Nightmare', seems fairly apropos.' A master of ironic observation, he suggests that although devices may be invented and bought to automatically illuminate one's bookshelves, 'no one has yet perfected any satisfactory device for illuminating homes where books are lacking. And consider for a moment, the infinite possibilities for enlightenment of a gadget for flashing red signals in the heads of all those who *need* to read a book!' In such a world, he suggests, he probably should 'offer some apology for a Catalogue devoted chiefly to *old* books; but being an antiquarian, I have a rather sentimental attachment to obsolescence.'

Summer fires often sweep across the forested hills and mountains of the Californian coastal ranges; Sowers wrote of his own experience in such a fire in Catalogue Sixty-one, in the early 1960s, remembering how he had worked to help extinguish a brush fire on his property some years earlier. 'I can recall the hot, spark-laden wind and our sweat and the frightening angry crackle as group after group of live-oaks flared and succumbed; I remember too the anxious vigil from our house roof, as great redwoods roared into candles flaming five hundred feet into the night sky! I like trees, and I hope never to see such a sight again.'

To Sowers, whose stock was, of course, particularly vulnerable, fire was a permanent worry. He had observed that much of the indigenous architecture of the area relied on adobe, a material whose weight, solidity and density make it relatively effective in surviving fires, and he decided to build an adobe book-room. Although he gives a much fuller description of the material, and of his use of it, later on, this project is first mentioned in Catalogue Thirty-two. 'In the early summer ... we experimented in a smallish way with adobe brick,' he writes. 'The first requirement of the process is a strong back – with or without a weak mind; and if I can manage that part, our next library building will be of that material. My friends in New York and other eastern points – some of whom I saw last spring – are inclined to be aghast at the amount of purely physical work attached to such an existence as this; but when I look out of the window of the average New York apartment, I wonder if even the proximity of the N.Y. Public Library and the Metropolitan Print Rooms could make such a prospect endurable.'

Sowers's name and trade were always associated with the world of the print, and with fine illustration generally, but neither he nor other booksellers can often have offered anything to match item 161 in Catalogue Thirty-three. It is *Toil*, a huge woodcut of a ploughman and two horses, with a Morris-like border, done in 1900 by William Strang and Robert Bryden. It consists of nine sheets of engraved wood, fitted together to make a print measuring five feet high by six. 'An interesting item for a large wall,' Sowers notes. The same catalogue is also notable for a collection of 135 Symbolist books by authors such as A.E. Coppard, Roy Campbell, HD (Hilda Doolittle), Ronald Firbank and Wyndham Lewis, among others. Symbolism was a late-nineteenth-century movement in French poetry, principally centred on the writing of Mallarmé and Verlaine, which began around 1880; symbolism was writing – but chiefly poetry – that sought to evoke a response in the reader through impression, intuition and sensation, rather than through description and narrative coherence. The movement was taken up strongly in Russia, where it was given an indigenous character, quite different from its French origins, and in Great Britain and America as well, where it took on the colours of the (largely) Anglo-Saxon frame of mind and diction, and lasted into the 1940s among some writers. The section is prefaced with an essay, 'Symbols in Literature' by Elinor Wylie, of whose books Sowers lists nineteen editions. By far the most interesting items offered, however, were works which we should not necessarily think of as being of only Symbolist interest. Katherine Mansfield's *The Dove's Nest and Other Stories*; Eugene O'Neill's *Mourning Becomes Electra*; a privately circulated collection of poems by Pound, with a portrait by Gaudier-Brzeska; and T.F. Powys's *The White Paternoster and Other Stories*. Collectors today might gladly decline the chance to buy the works of Wylie, Sylvia Townsend Warner or Edna St Vincent Millay that Sowers offered in this catalogue and instead pounce on the books named above or first editions of e.e. cummings's two earliest books, or Virginia Woolf's *Kew Gardens*, signed by the author and decorated by Vanessa Bell, especially at prices ranging from four to ten dollars.

In the early autumn of 1948, in Catalogue Thirty-eight, Sowers announces 'A new book by the Grabhorn Press.' This was his own third independent production as a publisher, *Early California Justice*, written by his new father-in-law, Judge George Cosgrave; it would survey nearly one hundred years of the work of the Federal District Court for the Southern District of California, from 1850 to 1944. Cosgrave had become a lawyer in 1895, and spent most of his career as a judge in Fresno. He died in 1945, so Sowers's book may have been intended partly as a memorial to him. Printed in an edition of four hundred copies, this hundred-page quarto volume was to sell at ten dollars following its publication on or about 15 November. Below the advertisement for it, on the same page of the catalogue, Sowers offers a great deal of the source material used in the book, together with Judge Cosgrave's typed manuscript, for a further fifty dollars, expressing the hope that the collection will find a home in a library or institution in the Los Angeles area. Perhaps he was thinking of the Huntington. It remained unsold, however, and was specifically excluded from the library of his own books that he offered to the University of California at Davis in February 1965.

Sowers's concern with the danger of forest fires is never far from his mind in the catalogues of this period, but he sees danger coupled with beauty. 'After a summer ending so dry it seemed that a sharp word might set the brush to burning,' he notes, 'and after the actual threat of serious fires not many miles away, a couple of light rains have made everyone in these mountains happy, and we breathe a sigh of relief. It is remarkable what the first rains in a dry country will do for us human beings. The woodland foliage is green again, with the summer dust washed off; the air is fresher and one is again aware of the sense of smell; it is pleasant to notice the distinctive aromas of hazel, oak, redwood or bay, which one had almost forgotten. But in addition to this, the rain seems to relieve a human nervous tension which is built up during a hot summer.'

Updating his readers on the construction of his adobe book-room, he reported that the building, measuring fifty-four by eighteen feet, now neared completion, 'despite the fact that it long looked to be a life-time occupation. With the roof partially on, torrential rains have three times soaked everything and compelled cessation of work – than which there can be few more exasperating tricks of the weather.' But now, he notes, 'the roof is on and the bulk of my stock has been moved in. However, the main Library room is still bare of shelving and likely to stay that way until after Christmas.'

Writing in 'a bit of Indian Summer, that beautiful, brief, most American of seasons,' he reflects that a 'taste for old books and prints is a mellow weakness which accords well with this mellow season. Despite the destruction of most of our California wines by the great advertising vintners, one can imagine the survival, here and there, of a few choice vintages, produced with the old care; and, despite the general preoccupation with money and the very dull present satisfactions which most money buys, it seems a good time to pour a little libation to the imaginary but golden past. It is a good time in which to re-read Fuller's 'Chevalier of Pensieri Vani'; (I wish someone would reprint it, or that someone would loan me a copy). And yes, it is also a good time to buy good books.'

Slightly out of chronological sequence, Catalogue Thirty-eight announces the publication of Catalogue Thirty-seven, which immediately followed it. Thirty-seven is notable for containing a two-part collection of titles in the history and literature of medicine, including alchemy, chemistry and botany. Sowers had become interested in the history of science and medicine, he wrote years later in Catalogue Sixty-one, while working at the Huntington, where he had been 'fascinated by the lore of the folio herbals of Gerard and Parkinson, with their hundreds of Woodcuts, and the other early English works of popular medicine, such as Elyot, Cogan, Langham and that perpetual best-seller Culpepper. Nor have I forgotten that more recently, curiously thumbing through a 16th century folio, I chanced on a recommendation of 'the moulde from stale bread for treatynge of greene woundes'. So old are all things new! (Ask me not chapter and verse!)'

Of the books he was offering in the first medical and scientific catalogue, he wrote: 'This list will have no popular appeal, and present indications are that printing costs will compel me to charge a dollar for it; but I expect the sales will be adequate to pay me something for my time; and the study of Medical History is proving a very stimulating experience.'

The first part was published in December 1948, and featured titles from A through L; the second completed the listings, which totalled, together, 467 items. These were the first of a number of his catalogues devoted to science and medicine. Clearly they represented a shift in Sowers's interests. From this point forward, modern literature accounts for less and less of his trade, as the evils of the mid-twentieth century preoccupy him more and more.

His introduction in the first part of Catalogue Thirty-seven sheds light, not only on the contents of the list, but also on the origins of

CATALOGVE XXXXI.

CHRISTMAS BOOKES *AND* PRINTS FOR COLLECTORS.

GLENWOOD, CALIFORNIA

Printed for Roy V. Sowers, Book-seller.

MDCCCCL .

his interest in antiquarian medical books and illustrations, and not a little on his career as a bookseller. 'It was during my service in the Huntington Library, some twenty years ago, that I was first intrigued by the little volumes on English Physick – Cogan's *Haven of Health*, Elyot's *Castel of Helth*, Langham's *Garden of Health*, and such like titles – and no less by the richly illustrated folio herbals of Gerard and Parkinson ... A little later, when I was making the usual mistakes of the young bookseller, I was fortunate in having a few clients who now and then put in a word for the classics of Science. The fact that this Catalogue includes a copy of the *Hortus Sanitatis* is probably due to the late Dr Casey Wood; the Isaac Newton manuscript and certain other personal extravagances of 10 or 15 years ago are the indirect result of the enthusiasm of Dr Horace Evans of Berkeley; and the motives of other acquisitions could be similarly traced ... On my buying trips to Europe, I met, here and there, many of the great booksellers and scholars, and a little of their understanding of great books – a very little perhaps – rubbed off. And it was my great good fortune to acquire, while they could be acquired, not a few books which are now excessively rare.'

He added: 'I recall that in 1936 I shortened my stay in Paris in order to be in England for the sale of the Newton Papers. Also, I heard that Sir D'Arcy Power had a duplicate copy of Harvey's *De Mortu Cordis*, and I wrote him about it. Thus, on a beautiful summer day in London, I left Sotheby's elated in the knowledge that I had secured a couple of Newton manuscripts, and went to have tea with the Librarian of the Royal College of Surgeons. The late Sir D'Arcy Power, even then was past eighty, and he talked of book collecting when he was young; also, he talked, almost with idolatry, of Sir William Osler. I did not get the Harvey volume, but it was a memorable afternoon ... In retrospect, that brief contact seems much more significant than most of my other preoccupations of that summer. For most of us, it is only the passage of the years that gives the perspective as to what matters and what does not. Sometimes, it seems that, as a bookseller, too much of my time has been devoted to the sale of trivia.'

Only a specialist could appreciate fully the depth and quality of the collection of science and medicine Sowers had put together for Catalogue Thirty-seven, but there are items even the generalist can appreciate: a second edition of Burton's *Anatomy of Melancholy*; titles by Sir Robert Boyle; John Gerard's famous *Herball*; Sir Thomas Elyot's aforementioned *Castel of Helth*; Elias Ashmole's *Theatrum Chemicum Britannicum*, 'containing severall Poeticall Pieces of our own English Philosophers, who have written the Hermetique Mysteries in their own Ancient Language ...' The last-named was of course the Ashmole whom Gunther described as 'the most remarkable antiquarian adventurer of the [seventeenth] century,' who gave an unheard-of legitimacy to modern scientific thought and went on to persuade the University of Oxford to build a centre for studies in Natural History and Chemistry, which would later bear his name as the Ashmolean Museum.

One of Sowers's busiest years was 1948. Not only did he publish the first of his catalogues of *materia medica* and his father-in-law's book about the history and characters of the Southern California bench but he was also working on an unpublished alchemical manuscript of Sir Isaac Newton's, which, he announced, was to appear in a limited edition (but never did). This information is found in footnote to 'Bookselling in the Mountains,' an article Sowers wrote for the Book Club of California's *Quarterly News-Letter*, a periodical to which he contributed regularly.

The appearance of the second half of the science and medicine catalogue coincided with an unusually hard time for the fruit farm. In the following spring, 1949, Sowers noted that 'it has been a Winter during which 'the simple life' has seemed peculiarly complicated. The inconveniences of the 'big freeze' – like most inconveniences – were due chiefly to our unpreparedness. With hundreds of feet of water pipe on top of the ground and unprotected, these pipes had to be drained to prevent freezing; and it is remarkable – to name only one dependency – how dependent we are on running water, and how much it complicates life to have to carry it, even for a few days.'

At this time, his spring catalogue still features his *Joan*, about which he writes modestly: 'Among Grabhorn productions it belongs with the group which includes the *Book of Ruth*, the Aesop, the Mandeville and the *Leaves of Grass*.' It should be noted that this opinion was not wholly objective, as neither Roderick Cave nor Joseph Blumenthal, in their important surveys of fine printing, mention *Joan* at all.

Christmas 1949 found Sowers in a Sowersian funk. 'I sometimes think it might be interesting to forget the catalogue,' he writes, 'and go to New England in search of that golden autumn which, in perfection, exists nowhere but in the paintings of Claude Lorraine; but eating is important, so, perforce, I trade a few books for bread.' From this lightly elegiac mood, he proceeds to one of his tirades about modern life. First he singles out the rapacity of the food-market capitalists who force him to sell pears for less than the cost of growing them. 'Should any readers wonder why they pay 40c or so, for a can of pears, for the contents of which the grower received 2c – well, this is mass marketing, untainted by any socialistic controls!' Having spent time reading the letters of Eric Gill, Sowers admits to sharing Gill's concern for the 'destruction of certain qualities in people … work, independence and self-reliance.' Specifically: 'The American farmer has been the last refuge of individuality in a nation that has forgotten it was founded by such individuals; and when mechanism has succeeded in destroying the personal qualities of our farmers – as it has already destroyed those of our city workers – we may expect consequences of which the least unpleasant will be hunger. We hereabouts can get along fairly happily without television, electric dishwashers – even without power saws for cutting firewood; but it would be exceedingly pleasant to be able once again to buy good wine, a piece of honest, non-synthetic cheese, or a loaf of bread that is fit to eat!'

Sowers even manages to wax dyspeptic in his catalogue notes. Writing of a commonplace book he has listed ('1803-1833, written in a very neat small hand'), he notes that decent penmanship 'has now become so rare that such a volume as this charms, on this score alone …'. Also, 'a brief sampling of the matter written by this unknown author leaves me in some doubt as to the superior taste of our own times.'

The modern world was coming up fast on Sowers's blind side, for in his next catalogue he experiments for the first time with photographs to illustrate his offerings, although, as he admits, most of the half-tones 'are inadequate, but they may serve better than words in conveying the appearance of Prints and Bindings.' He promises more in subsequent catalogues, and 'more skilfully prepared.'

Number Forty-one was his only catalogue in 1950: a Christmas catalogue of books and prints once again, addressed from Parnassus Hill Ranch, Glenwood. Sowers uses the introduction to reflect on the lessons he has learned from the year's harvest in this, 'the 13th year I have owned this pear orchard, and since the 1950 crop was a complete failure, I could make the obvious deduction of ill luck; however, I now regard my orchard activities as part of my education; and last year with a 40-ton crop, I lost nearly as much as I did this year with none.... I have been interested to learn that Emerson also had at Concord a pear orchard to which he was devoted. Reading between the lines of his *Journals*, I conclude that he also found his trees exacting of effort and recalcitrant of results. On one occasion he was waited upon by a group of men from the local agricultural fair, asking to see his orchard; and his bosom swelled with pride, – until they informed him that they were curious to see the trees which could produce pears with so many things wrong with them. Periodically I threaten to tear out my orchard. But since the first rains, the trees, having failed of any golden fruit, have turned their leaves to gold, – gold and crimson, bright as any eastern maples; and as I walked through them today, I thought perhaps I'd wait another year before pulling them out.'

Early in 1952, the Sowerses went to buy books in Britain and Europe, staying away eight months. Just before their return to California from 'London's manifold distractions,' Sowers issued a four-page list of books picked up during the trip. Slim it may have been, but the simple pamphlet ran to 182 items, including a first edition of Sir William Davenant's *Works* (1673), a first edition of *Tess of the*

D'Urbervilles, three fine books from the Nonesuch Press and a group of seven Robert Louis Stevenson firsts. From this standpoint in time, however, Arthur Waley's influential *A Hundred and Seventy Chinese Poems*, in the handsome Chiswick Press edition, at only three dollars, would be more likely to attract disproportionate attention, for Charles Whittingham's Chiswick Press had a reputation, in times of general depravity in English printing, as one of the foremost jobbing shops in the kingdom. Whittingham and his partner, William Pickering, had revived Caslon's beautiful old English typeface in 1844. Chiswick was, quite naturally, the press to which William Morris turned for the printing of his first books, the ones on which the Arts and Crafts Movement was founded.

The London list was printed for Sowers by the firm of Robert Stockwell Ltd of South London, and was posted from there. On future trips to England he would employ the firm the same way.

Something of the flavour of that trip, and of its importance to Sowers, can be deduced from his essay 'The Durham Cathedral Library,' published in the spring 1953 issue of the *Quarterly News-Letter*. Sowers recalled that he and Margaret 'visited, in addition to hundreds of book shops, a number of the older libraries, both in Britain and on the continent. I was a librarian before I was a bookseller; and I have long felt that the history of Western civilization could well be written in terms of the history of libraries. The subject is an humbling one …' The tribute to Durham Cathedral itself is a masterpiece of elegant, discursive, informative prose, in which the author's obvious enchantment with that particular piece of history is conveyed to the reader most feelingly.

Catalogue Fifty, appearing in 1953, still carried a Glenwood address and a Santa Cruz telephone number. (Sowers had proudly announced the latter – 'Line newly installed: Santa Cruz 102-J-2' – in the previous catalogue, which had been an impressive listing of more than sixty titles by or about Robert Boyle and Sir Isaac Newton.) Overprinted on the cover of Fifty was the rubber-stamped phrase '25,000 Mt Charley Road.' Inside were his reflections on an important anniversary: 'it is just 25 years since I left the relative security of the Huntington Library to enter bookselling: and after having several city bookshops, my business is now conducted by mail from a remote hill-top ranch in the Santa Cruz mountains.... we live on a dirt road, which was probably a better road in 1860 than it is today. It is called Mountain Charlie [*sic*] Road, after the pioneer local character who built it, with Irish immigrant labour, about 1858.' The road followed a ridge 'trod by the Franciscan fathers between the missions of Santa Clara and Santa Cruz.' The eponymous Mountain Charley was one Charles Henry McKiernan, who, though not responsible for construction of the road, became a dashing and noted stage-coach driver along its length for many years. He is not to be confused with another stage driver of that area and period, Cock-eye Charley Parkhurst, whose death in 1879 brought to light the unexpected intelligence that Cock-eye Charley was a female who, voting in her masquerade as a man, had consequently been the first woman to exercise the franchise in California.

Sowers goes on to recall how, despite the challenges and stimuli of city life, he grew weary of its bureaucratic and personal demands, noting in characteristic manner that 'the normal pattern of American business in our cities has little room for the individual. Salesmanship is a bore, and bookselling, despite its name, should be more nearly a profession than a business.' Up in the hills, he adds, 'I sell perhaps one quarter of the books which I could sell in a city location, but I don't have to worry about rent, nor about the problem of finding assistants who know French from Latin.' By now, his catalogues were selling out. 'Very occasionally,' he writes, 'some serious collector or librarian pays me a visit by appointment; but in the main I work by correspondence.' The rarity of such visits might well be explained by his acknowledgement that Mountain Charley Road was 'rough, and narrow, and full of twists ... impassable in heavy rains.' Another drawback was the fact that many did not find Sowers a warm and inviting personality. Perhaps the rural life, however poetically Sowers might describe it at times, contributed to this side of his character.

In a letter to Charles Antin in the 1980s, Margaret Sowers noted,

'The setting, however idyllic, carried the threat of fires during the long, dry summers as well as that of thieves and vandals in the absence of near neighbors,' though the fire danger, at least, was reduced by completion of the adobe book-room in 1951, when Sowers took the opportunity to reflect on what had been achieved. 'During those strenuous five years I learned a lot about adobe, because I had to. I even began by making a couple of hundred of my own bricks, but this I soon abandoned as requiring a stronger back than mine. Nowadays, when friends comment on the beauty of the obviously hand work – and it is a beautiful building – I find myself thinking of the fact that those bricks weigh 50 lbs. apiece, and I wonder how I ever managed to put up the foot-thick walls.' As he wrote in another of his catalogue essays, 'Free men have always used their hands to create for their own needs.'

Catalogue Fifty contains photographs of Sowers in the adobe structure amid piles and piles of books brought home from Europe in 1951. 'The confusion is about normal,' he writes of the scene, with its orderly but multitudinous stacks of books covering the tables and the floor. 'There still aren't enough shelves for all the books, so some of the European purchases of two years ago remain in parcels yet unopened. In due course, it is hoped, these books will be unpacked, repaired where necessary, catalogued, sold, repacked and mailed; and the proprietor ... with the help of his long-suffering wife, will do it all.' Of himself, seen in the accompanying photographs trying to sort the books, he says, 'That is the proprietor, not the office-boy!'

By now it should be clear that the one most outstanding characteristic of Roy Vernon Sowers was his utter contempt for the age in which he lived and its meretricious and venal values. In catalogue after catalogue – in his descriptions of books as often as in the essays – he inveighs against the ignorance, greed and cupidity of the times, never losing a chance to take a pot-shot at politicians, educators, university and library administrators and the cultural values that, he thought, characterized post-war society. Bernard Rosenthal, a member of the famous bookselling family in Berkeley, knew Sowers and mentions him in the obituary of his father, Erwin Rosenthal, in *AB*

Bookman's Weekly in 1982, where he sums up Sowers's dispute with the twentieth century: 'There was Roy Vernon Sowers, living in the wild hills of Los Gatos, at the improbable address of 25,000 Mountain Charlie [*sic*] Road, a man of Walpole's time, born in the wrong century and in the wrong country and forever aware of it (the prefaces to his catalogues, lamenting the onset of the twentieth century or, for that matter, of the nineteenth, were famous in their time).'

Sowers never tried to disguise or hide his distaste for the contemporary world and its other inhabitants. 'Returning from our last visit to Europe,' he notes in Catalogue Fifty, 'I could not help noticing how much alike most Americans look – both men and women. Partly this is a rather boresome, too well-dressed prosperity; but partly, I fear, it is the reflection of uniform minds. Almost, one can list the books they have read – by listing the book club publications of recent years.' In a similar vein: 'I don't think much of the Marxian emphasis on pure materialism. Man has to earn his livelihood, but he also has to live and feel and think. And a house full of gadgets still doesn't make an empty mind any more stimulating to live with. One of the good things that can be said of the Depression of the thirties, is that despite the scars it left, some of us at least learned what we could do without.' So it was, then, that in 'this anniversary catalogue I have listed some great Books and some very great Prints, including such names as Blake, Breughel, Dürer and Rembrandt. These are for people with minds and with cultivated tastes; and for such, they are not necessarily luxuries. Some of you, like ourselves, may drive a 12-year-old car, belong to no country club, and get along without television (quite happily!). So, as the proverb goes, each to his taste.' And yet, faced with the beauty of his surroundings and his essential good nature (yes or, as he would write, with his addiction to exclamation points, 'Yes!'), as well as with his overriding sense of the primacy of other, more important, even timeless things, he could not quite surrender himself to being a dreary reiterator of old woes and time-worn prejudices. Recalling his boyhood in Ontario, to which he frequently referred in describing his mountain home, particularly in the autumn, he continues: 'Here, we don't have the maples, nor the hickory, but there is the same haze in the air and the same mellow sunlight, like a benediction. The pressure of harvest past, one savours the frost in a cluster of grapes overlooked by the birds, and enjoys a couple of late and sweet sun-dried prunes in the fallen golden leaves beneath the trees. It is good to pause and look at the distant hills and soak up this mellow autumn weather. A light rain has washed the summer dust from the leaves, and in the woods one can smell again the aroma of hazel, bay and yerba buena. Another rain will probably bring up the mushrooms. And, as I glance up at the immensity of some of our centuries-old redwoods, I am reminded that all this has happened before. Because most of Time is the Past. The Sadeler engravings of 'The Months' listed herein, and done in 1607, show the apples being picked, the grapes being crushed, the leaves falling and the nuts being gathered. So, century after century, generations of men have worked, loved, fought, drunk the wine, played the fool and lived and died; but some of them have also had dreams. And most of their dreams are in Books, or in their Art that has survived. Perhaps as the year draws to its close it is natural to think a bit of the Past. So, after preparing the catalogue, after living, if but briefly, with a couple of hundred Books and Prints which are part of the noble harvest of five centuries, one senses maybe something of the greatness we inherit. Let us pour a little libation to the dreams of great men of other days; and may the good Lord forgive me for selling these things for money!'

Sowers and his wife returned to Europe to travel and buy books, landing at Rome on New Year's Day 1952. Sowers remarked that 'it is perhaps typical of this city of contrasts that as we stepped from the modern enormity of Mussolini's railroad station we should be faced by the ruins of Servius Tullius of the third century BC.'

These and other remarks preface another list of medical and scientific books (Catalogue Fifty-one), although much of this essay is taken up with a remarkable account of the Hospital of Santo Spirito and the great medical library it houses. His inspection of the historic hospital itself arose from a visit to the Bibliotheca Lancisiana, 'a lofty room with beautiful bookcases lining the walls and with access to the upper tier by an inconspicuous balcony. The woodwork is beautifully carved, the books are behind glass, and the floor space ... is largely occupied by a pair of large spheres, a marble bust of Lancisi, and glass cases containing anatomical and mathematical instruments.' Lancisi, 'the greatest Italian clinician of his time,' was physician to Pope Clement XI and founded the library in 1714 by donating his own collection of twenty thousand scientific and medical books to Santo Spirito 'for the benefit of the students and doctors there.' Sowers was surprised when, after having enjoyed a tour of the small library with the librarian, Pietro de Angelis, the latter threw open a small door at eye level, giving Sowers a bird's-eye view of the interior of the great hospital, with its rows and rows of beds and patients.

Describing the hospital and its history, Sowers uses the opportunity to reflect on the early history of hospitals, medicine and European culture. The English king, John, whom legend accuses of losing the crown jewels while fleeing across the Wash, endowed it with an annual stipend in 1207. Leonardo da Vinci studied anatomy there briefly, but fell foul of the Pope over accusations of body-snatching. John Evelyn, that robust antiquarian, visited the hospital in 1645 and wrote of it approvingly.

The overwhelming sense of cultural memory that the place evoked, Sowers recalled, resulted in their 'exhausting [ourselves] in the vain effort to encompass 2500 years of time past ...' Recalling Jasper Schad's opinion, that Sowers never seemed to be a completely happy man, and remembering also Bernard Rosenthal's kindly observation about him, the reader is left in no doubt as to where, and in what epoch, Sowers would have felt most contented and at home.

‹ *Winding Down* ›

THE LAST BOOK in which Sowers had a hand in publishing was the *Chronology of 25 Years at The Roxburghe Club of San Francisco*, which he edited. It appeared in 1954 and contained introductions by himself and Carl Wheat, an old friend in the rare book trade in California. Wheat had been one of the club's founders in 1928, along with Robert Grabhorn, the photographer Ansel Adams and the brilliantly innovative typographer Karl Klingspor. The *Chronology* was printed by the Grabhorn Press and can be found in the second volume of the Grabhorn bibliography.

In 1955, Sowers undertook another visit to Europe, where he and his wife visited the Bodleian Library in Oxford, the Bibliothèque Nationale in Paris and a number of other major libraries in England and France before moving on to ones in Italy, a country he found 'always beautiful and always exhausting.' Sowers had long wanted to see 'some monastic libraries which had survived the centuries without the wholesale [des]spoilation … associated with Henry VIII in England, the French Revolution, and with the unification of Italy …' To accomplish this, the couple drove from Italy through Yugoslavia to Austria, to visit the monastic library at Admont, in the Styrian Alps, which was founded by the Benedictines in 1074 (and preserves a list of its librarians since 1140). Admont had been suppressed under Hitler, Sowers notes, and its books removed for storage to Dachau, where they were liberated at the end of the war by the US army, 'though the Dachau stamp remains in them …'

A disquisition on Admont, and the meaning and value of such a library, inevitably leads Sowers to an oblique comparison between Old and New World values. He concludes that there is so much work 'waiting to be done in so many old-world libraries [that] if we could send a few of our students to help, what they would learn would be of more significance to the future of our own libraries than anything they might miss in our usual library schools.'

The Sowerses were back in Europe again in June 1957, and their visit to the medical school at Montpellier in France forms the basis of the introduction to Catalogue Fifty-seven, which, once again, is largely devoted to medicine and science (there were to be six more yet). The catalogue was once again printed for him while he was staying in England, by Stockwell's in London, with copies posted both from England and the United States.

Montpellier is the second-oldest medical school in Europe, Sowers observes (the one at Salerno is the oldest). Rabelais was a student at Montpellier, although when he registered on 1 September 1530 he was already a mature and well-educated monk in the Benedictine order (having transferred from the Franciscans because they opposed his studies). How much more advanced he was than his fellow students can be deduced from the fact that he completed three years' study in only one year, receiving his bachelor's degree in December 1531. Sowers ranges widely over science, medicine and society during the Renaissance period in the course of this engaging essay, taking the opportunity to share – and yes, display – his general erudition and vast store of arcane knowledge of the book world. But how can we cavil when he describes a public dissection directed by Rabelais at the school in 1538? 'By modern standards this must have been a curious spectacle. The room was heavy with incense, in an attempt to overcome the less pleasant odors, and in addition to the students and their masters, Rabelais had invited a number of beautiful women of Montpellier who were present, wearing masks. The body was that of a criminal who had been hanged, and there is extant a poem by Etienne Dolet, congratulating the corpse on signal service to his fellow men after his useless life, in being the subject of such a learned exposition. It is a sad commentary on the times that this great printer and scholar – who, incidentally, printed editions of Rabelais – was himself to be publicly burned for heresy in Paris eight years later. For this lecture on anatomy, Rabelais received a gold piece from the Dean of the school, Jean Scurron.' Sowers remembers how, on leaving the school after his visit, he noted how unprepossessing a place it looked, despite its more than one thousand years of history. 'In our own country,' he writes, 'such a School, with such a history, would have administrators and public relations staff and buildings and a speech-making president to raise an endowment of a hundred million dollars; but would it be a better School? Then we drove out of town, pausing briefly for a glimpse of the nearby Botanical Garden, the oldest in France; and as we headed north again over the hot and rocky plain, I looked at the close-pruned olive trees and the little vineyards and wondered how one is to judge what is important.'

Sowers's curmudgeonly disaffection with the present is always related to his perception of society's rush to embrace the lowest common denominator of commercialization and to the lack of civility and loss of a sense of history and community this entails. But often his disgusted resignation at what he sees happening all around him hides a prescience and understanding of important issues about quality of life that louder and more insistent protesters were to discover later on. Catalogue Sixty presents an excellent example of Sowers as the voice in the wilderness. The catalogue is devoted to transportation and technology, surely subjects in which Sowers was supremely and constitutionally uninterested, and its essay is entitled, ominously, 'Foreword – and Lament.' Having testified to the poignant beauty of his farm in the autumn, he turns on his habitual quarry, modern society. 'To some of us, these unimportant things of beauty seem very important; and it is sad to have the testimony from all parts of our land of the swallowing of our countryside by industrialism, highways and suburbia. Unlike power and oil, conservation has no Washington lobby. The youth of today … might well pause to ask what of our heritage of natural beauty will remain for their children if they continue to sanction the government philosophy of the Hell's canyon give-away. If eternal vigilance is the price of liberty, then I suspect this will be known to future generations as the era of 'The Great Sleep'. If you love hills and streams and forests and the open spaces, look now; because soon they will be no more.' And of the books in the catalogue, he observes how 'paradoxically, in an age of jet-plane travel, it may be positively stimulating to our jaded imaginations to live with an old Print of a sailing ship, or of a Mail Coach and straining horses; or to read of the human skills which went into production and handicraft before we became so totally obsessed with machinery.'

If Sowers achieved great renown in his lifetime, it was limited to his peers in the book trade, and to his knowledgeable clients, who knew a master when they were in the presence of one, even if only on the printed page. Whenever his essays are mentioned, however, the one invariably called to mind first is that which introduces Catalogue Sixty-one. Commentators have tended to name it 'Rain,' although he himself gave it the title 'Mushrooms – and Other Things of Little Consequence.' I quote from it for no better reason than that it is the most cogent example of Sowers's writing, combining as it does his easily worn erudition, his love of tradition and his keen understanding of, and relationship with, the natural world:

'Well ... it was raining; and as rain blots out distance, so I became more aware of the terrain near at hand. As I started down, my feet sank in the deep leaf mold, still dry in spots, and the redolence of California summer rose around me, – the dusty smells of fallen leaves, oak and poison oak, Madrone and Mazanita and hazel, – and with it, also, the damp and pleasant odour of leaf decay, the promise of mushrooms and much else.'

Ever the Don Quixote, tilting at windmills, Sowers next turns his impatient attention on radio and television. To Canadians, brought up with the Canadian Broadcasting Corporation, and consequently always in the throes of a debate about what public radio and television is worth, Sowers's arguments will sound familiar, even if few have expressed them with his withering contempt. In Catalogue Sixty-two, spreading himself from a learned disquisition about the origins of Johnny Appleseed to the pleasures of winter and enforced indoor activity such as listening to music, he considers the broadcast media and finds them wanting. 'As a free American,' he writes, 'I resent moronic television advertising; and were the few good programmes ten times as many, the price would still be too high. I feel almost as strongly about the prostitution of our commercial radio; and our recent installation of an FM set, tuned to non-commercial Berkeley KPFA has given us a taste of what American radio could be – a powerful, civilizing influence, as is the BBC in Britain. KPFA is one of the few bright spots in the contemporary scene, and any Californian who believes in freedom (not just the word!) should try to tune in ... and subscribe the ten dollars a year to keep them going. In passing it seems to me that the long obvious failures of American education are chiefly due to the climate of general American public opinion. That climate, of amused contempt for solid learning of any sort, has been consistently cultivated over our commercial airways and it has to be corrected.'

Although not given to much examination of the details of his own life, beyond where the depredations of an uncivilized and crass society impinged on it and demanded a rejoinder, Sowers became more and more reflective as he grew older, using his essays to reminisce about the book trade and the people he had known and to provide insights into the kind of life he had led and the forces that had shaped and governed it, even as he fell victim time and again to the gloomy impulse to disparage the society in which he found himself marooned.

The Sowerses spent a year travelling in Europe between the summers of 1962 and 1963, during much of which time Sowers laboured on a bibliography of medicine and science at libraries in London and in the Bodleian at Oxford, where he had the unmitigated pleasure of working with the greatest medical bibliography ever published, that of Sir William Osler, surrounded by works by Hippocrates, Galen, Charles Estienne and Theophrastus, among others, and the herbals of Gerard and Parkinson, his favourites. Sowers was a frequent visitor to the Bodleian and mentions it in a number of essays. That he loved to be there is conveyed nowhere more succinctly than in Catalogue Seventy, issued on his return to America. He and Margaret had enjoyed Italy, Sicily and France, he declared, but were glad to settle at

BIOLIO-GALLIMAUFRY II.

CATALOGUE XXV

ST. AUGUSTINE · BASKERVILLE · SYMONS · COLOURED PLATES. · BLADES · ASTRONOMY · COMPLEAT ANGLER · BOSWELL · MILITARY · PHILOSOPHY · *Limited Editions* · DE QUINCEY · PATER · BRONTE. · COOKERY · JAPANESE COLOUR PRINTS · FINE PRINTING · UPDIKE · SAN FRANCISCO · SPINOZA · SHAKESPEARE · AMERICA. · ROMANCES · SWINBURNE · MINIATURES · POETRY · LAW · HERALDRY. · HOLY BIBLE · AMATORY · DONNE · DANIEL PRESS · MARY QUEEN OF SCOTS · Costume

ADVENTURE · SUETONIUS · *Library Sets* · MORRIS · PEPYS · ELIOT · MOSHER · SCOTLAND · Tobacco · LILLY · MAPS · HISTORY · ERASMUS · FURNITURE · CURWEN PRESS · Classics · ARCTIC · FIRST EDITIONS · BINDING. · ART · Virgil · PLAYS · VIERGE

CALIFORNIANA · THEATRE · ESSAYS

BOOKS

MEZZOTINTS · PHOTOGRAPHY · EGYPT · A'KEMPIS · ROWLANDSON · ASTROLOGY · BYRON · GOSSE · CARROLL · WILKINS · STEVENSON · GALSWORTHY · BIOGRAPHY · COURT MEMOIRS · Travel · BROWNING · ADDISON · Literature · BUTLER · ARTHUR RACKHAM · ETC. · BACON · QUEEN VICTORIA · Medical · HORSES. · SPORT · DÜRER · NATURAL HISTORY · HUSBANDRY · Bibliography · DOVES PRESS · Print Collecting · WHITMAN · DE FOE · MEYNELL · CRUIKSHANK · GRABHORN PRESS · BLAKE · WITCHCRAFT · ETCHINGS. · TYPOGRAPHY · ANON. · LAMB · EARLY PRINTING · SWIFT · LUCRETIUS · BOOKPLATES · SHAW · LUCIAN · Judaica · ARCHITECTURE. · ESTIENNE · CHEMISTRY & PHYSICS

1940 · FIVE HUNDRED YEARS OF PRINTING

ROY VERNON SOWERS

117 MONTGOMERY ST. [EXbrook 5686] SAN FRANCISCO

last 'for happy months in Oxford, reading in the Bodleian and seeing the gardens, particularly the Old Botanic Garden, in all their moods from earliest spring blossom to autumn fruit and frost ...'. His catalogue for March 1964 indicates he has become the agent in the US and Canada for the official *Illuminated Manuscript Treasures of the Bodleian Library, Oxford* on 35mm colour filmstrips, available at $1,082, at an exchange rate of $2.80 to the pound sterling.

Clive Hurst, head of special collections at the Bodleian, quoting an entry about Sowers as a library benefactor in a small Oxford publication, remarks: 'Towards the end of his life, [Sowers] seriously considered coming to live here. This did not materialise and he died in California. Under the terms of his will, the Bodleian was to be allowed to select anything it wanted from his collection of books and prints, the remainder of which would then be sold for the Library's benefit. [The Bodleian] finally received over one hundred and fourteen thousand dollars from the estate, in addition to more than fourteen thousand dollars which Mr Sowers had given during his lifetime.' The income supports the Sowers Fund, which amounted to thirteen thousand dollars in 1995, used to buy antiquarian books and manuscripts.

In Catalogue Seventy, after rhapsodizing about the history, culture and timelessness of Oxford, Sowers rails against the encroachment on his beloved Santa Cruz hills of suburbia, with its 'plaster ducks ... and the inevitable barbecue-pit in the background.' He bemoans the future predicted by the 'dirty smog of the industrialized Santa Clara valley' and the 'planned obsolescence of US big business.' About books and literacy, he despairs at what we would call, today, the dumbing-down of the American reader, to whom books are as expendable as 'last week's issue of *Time* magazine.' Perhaps intimations of mortality were beginning to bedevil him at this time. He was in his mid-sixties now and felt himself ever more at odds with, and out of place in, the world. In his next catalogue, he confesses that his chief regrets, 'like those of all elderly booksellers – are for books I should not have sold.' He then goes on to make reference, for the first time in an introductory essay, to selling books from his own collection, offering 'some prizes which have been cherished personally, some of them for ten or twenty years or more . . .' He was winding down.

In a number of subsequent catalogues, Sowers would offer rich vignettes of his life in rare books, ones full of a fascinating erudition and witty gossip. He writes in Catalogue Seventy-three: 'How many books I have handled, in bookshops, auction rooms and libraries, here and abroad – during the past 35 years, I cannot guess; but probably at least 500 for every one which I have actually bought and sold. And from them chiefly has come such book-knowledge as I have . . .'. Introducing yet another catalogue of medicine and science, he states that the books described 'represent a field of interest so limitless that the years of Methuseleh would not suffice to exhaust it. All of them are uncommon, and many of such rarity as to make the ordinary use of the term seem ridiculous; but their real importance is not rarity, but content.'

As if the essays in his catalogues of the 1960s were not evidence enough that Sowers was preparing to retire, there were his several attempts to negotiate the sale of his library to one or other of the university libraries in California; in addition, he also gave away important books to deserving recipients. In January 1965, he had a letter from D.T. Clark, librarian at the University of California at Santa Cruz, thanking him for his gift of a scarce copy of J. Sanderson's 1884 book, *Ocean Cruise and Deep Water Regatta of the Pacific Yacht Club.* 'We particularly welcome this notable addition to our growing regional history collection,' Clark wrote, 'and because of its colorful lithographs of [a] Santa Cruz connected event, the book will have an honored place.'

Shortly afterwards, in February, Sowers began to negotiate for the disposal of both his private library and his stock-in-trade. He corresponded with Richard Blanchard, university librarian at the University of California at Davis, with a suggestion that the books be divided among several of the different UC campuses. Sowers's summary of the contents of his private library and stock came to 7,318 books, which he valued at $114,800 in 1965 dollars. The list included seven hundred volumes on the history of medicine, early science and technology; 175 early non-English books from 1478-1800; 325 English books prior to 1701, including twenty important English Bibles; three hundred volumes of eighteenth-century English literature; a thousand books of later English literature and criticism and modern American and British firsts; three thousand volumes of miscellaneous bibliography, art, illustrated books, fine press books, Americana and examples of fine binding; 680 volumes of recently catalogued items; one hundred volumes of Greek and Latin classics printed before 1800; 110 on wine or cookery; plus 'a large collection of booksellers and book auction catalogues, 1927 to 1963. Some thousands.' In the accompanying letter, Sowers explained why he was willing to dispose of his library this way. 'I estimate that it will require two full years of my time to liquidate my collection by Catalogue and by auction,' he wrote. 'Time which I would prefer to devote to certain long-postponed writing and editing projects.' He concluded that if all went ahead as he wished it might, then he would be in a position 'to make substantial gifts to one of the University Libraries ...'

But nothing came of the attempted sale to Davis. So in December 1965, Sowers prepared another list, detailing a small bequest to the library of the University of California at Santa Cruz. It consisted of books, historic stock certificates, magazine caricatures, letters, etc., and included an 1897 edition of Samuel Clemens's *Following the Equator, A Journey around the World*. By the autumn of 1966, the offer of his entire private library and business stock had shifted to the university library at Santa Cruz. On 16 September, Sowers, who was in Europe again, wrote to Donald T. Clark from Soglio in Switzerland with a brief outline of his collecting reminiscences which Clark appears to have asked him to compose, perhaps as a prefatory essay to a published account of Sowers's benefaction (and indeed it appeared, as 'A Bookseller Reminisces,' in the Spring 1967 number of *Quarterly News-Letter*). He wrote:

'When, after some thirty years of collecting books, one arrives at the stage of relinquishing them, it is difficult to avoid reminiscences because a library itself constitutes a sort of personal history of its owner. Handling these volumes for the last time, I am reminded not only of my own early bookish enthusiasms, of book-hunting pleasures and disappointments, but above all, of the many great and wise booksellers, European and American, who have helped me make this collection.

'English Literature, Book Illustrations, and Typography are the three fields chiefly represented in this library, and as is frequently the case its development was, in a sense, history in reverse. At the beginning, as a very young bookseller, I shared the enthusiasms of my contemporaries for the work of my own generation – for Galsworthy, Shaw, Hemmingway [*sic*] etc. and the poets of the 20s – and how sure I was that I could spot true genius! Later, by way of Dickens, Thackeray, Trollope and Shelley, I began to appreciate the 19th century; and then the 18th, and ultimately, when I progressed to the Elizabethans I felt that I was touching reality. At all stages of this peregrination into our literary past, books of criticism and reference were acquired, many of them still unread by me; for an active bookseller generally knows the books to be read in any field, even if he has little time for reading himself. Coincidentally, my interest in Book Illustration was growing. From such well-known artists as Arthur Rackham, Hugh Thomson, Joseph Pennell and Lovat Fraser, I found my enthusiasms moving backwards in time, to the Bewicks, to William Blacke [*sic*] to the beginnings of colour-plate work, to the early engravers and finally to the woodcut masterpieces of the age of Albrecht Dürer. Each stage in this journey was one of discovery – of new skills and scarcely imagined techniques.

'It was during my earliest days at the Huntington Library that I began to appreciate modern fine printing subsequent to that of the Kelmscott Press. This was the period of the great work of the Nonesuch press in England and of the Grabhorns in America – to name only two of many. Indeed, it was the golden age of the private press, and one has but to refer to Tomkinson or Ransom to realise that the 20s and 30s, both in Europe and America, somehow fertilised enormous accomplishments in type and book design. Any collector of the time was bound to be interested in typography, and again, the more he knew of modern work, the more inevitably he was led to seek examples of the printers of the 15th and 16th centuries.

'Fortunately or otherwise, a private library is seldom the product of any logical plan, it grows according to the knowledge and enthusiasms – not to mention the means – of its owners. All collectors perpetually regret the books they did not buy. I once passed up a 1613 Champlain's *Voyages* in Paris for want of $15, and I can recall many other similar lost opportunities, but that $15 in 1926 was as inaccessible to me as Harvey's 1628 *De Mortu Cordis* is to the poor medical student of today, and this is as it should be. If Caxtons, Shakespeare Quartos, and Ashendene Dantes were to be found in any bookshop, most of the pleasure and excitement of book collecting would vanish. Great books have a way of becoming rare, but quite aside from rarity, the building of a library is a constant exercise in discrimination, knowledge and taste, and every collector – unless he be a mere accumulator – comes to feel that in certain areas at least, he has superior knowledge.

'By general standards a library of 5,000 volumes is quite substantial, and yet in terms of bookish interests for half a century of mature and varied life, it represents only two books a week – not necessarily books one has read, but also those one *hopes* to read – even those beautiful examples on hand made paper and in fine bindings which one will always keep immaculate (to the scorn, of course, of the philistinic general public!)

'In our time, when, along with virtual extinction of fine typography, there is an increasing tendency, especially among the young, to cast aside older standards of taste and excellence, both in art and in literature, one cannot be too optimistic as to the survival of any books. The mood of the day seems to be that not of men but merely of machines. In place of centuries-old hard won standards of cultivation above the human norm, we see everywhere the new barbarism of taste dictated by the mass-mind. Whether or not our universities can successfully resist this pressure to surrender to mediocrity, it is

CATALOGUE XXXIII.

ROY VERNON SOWERS
FINE & RARE BOOKS
GLENWOOD, CALIFORNIA

still too early to say; but in seeing my books in the Library of the new Santa Cruz campus of the University of California, it is my hope that a few of them may survive the current wave of anti-intellectualism in America and that among new generations of students, a few may be inspired by them to the old standards of cultivation and accomplishment, rather than to mere mechanisation.'

To which he added a postscript: 'We are high in the Swiss mountains at a pleasant but simple pension and I have no typewriter and little in the way of paper. I hope this is somewhat along the lines you want – if not, don't use it. Cut if necessary. Best regards, RVS.'

Two years later, in his last contribution to the *Quarterly News-Letter*, he would write: 'In this probably final listing of Books & Prints from my personal collection I am tempted to a few backward glances at parting from them. Always more a collector than a bookseller, as I now realise, I ask myself why.' This essay was also the preface to Catalogue Seventy-nine, his last. Under the heading 'Recollections and Prejudices,' he looks back over his life as a dealer in rare books and prints, the people he met and the wonderful libraries his work had required him to visit. As so often before, he uses the essay to draw sharp and disadvantageous contrasts with contemporary life and mores, the present poverty of language and imagination and the want of civility. Tired, out-of-sorts with life and society, he takes refuge in that which has been his life's passion: the beauty and serenity of books. He concludes, at last, with grace, referring to the timelessness of the joy of fine books to draw the essay, and his career as one of North America's great bibliophiles and antiquarians, to a close: 'As a book-lover and an orchidist of sort, I have long enjoyed reading in the earlier writers on gardening and agriculture – Hill, Blagrave, Meager, Markham, Evelyn and Worlidge – not to mention Virgil's *Georgics* and that modern masterpiece, Sackville-West's *The Land*. Such books, as we know, were the familiars of Jefferson and the founding fathers, but also, Horace, Plato, Bacon, Harrington, Locke and Hobbes. And I can scarcely end more gracefully than with Abraham Cowley's introductory words to Evelyn's *Sylva*: 'I have never had any other desire so strong and so like to Covetousness, as that one which I have had always, that I might be Master at last of a small House and a large Garden, with very moderate Conveniences joined to them, and there dedicate the Remainder of my Life only to the culture of them, and Study of Nature."

One more piece of writing followed, an unlikely one in many ways and also one that Sowers did not live to see in print. He wrote an essay about the Swiss-born British poet Arthur Cravan, who claimed to be the nephew of Oscar Wilde and to have deserted from seventeen different armies. The sixteen-page book was published posthumously, in 1984, as *My Friend Aristide*, for distribution to the members of California's two foremost book-lovers' associations, the Roxburghe Club of San Francisco and the Zamorano Club of Los Angeles.

Towards the end of his life, Sowers became quite frail, having suffered from arterial sclerosis for about ten years. He began to make plans to sell the ranch and move to Vancouver, a city he had visited and found very congenial; Margaret had cousins there who would have given them entree into Vancouver society. But on 12 November 1970 he had a massive cerebral haemorrhage while he was dressing for breakfast. He died within minutes.

‹ *Selected Bibliography* ›

Antin, Charles. 'A Rare Bookman and His Catalogues,' *AB Bookman's Weekly*, 13 February 1984.

Cave, Roderick. *The Private Press*. New York: R.R. Bowker, 1983.

Rosenthal, Robert. 'Two Cities, Two Bibliophiles,' in *A Bibliophiles's Los Angeles – Essays for the International Association of Bibliophiles*. Los Angeles, 1985.

Schad, Robert O. 'La Miniatura Used for Young Artists' (obituary of Alice Millard), Los Angeles *Times*, 16 July 1938.

Simpson, Edmund E., ed. *An Excerpt from the Book Catalogues of Roy Vernon Sowers*. Placerville, California: The Blackwood Press, 1980.

Sowers, Roy Vernon. 'A Bookseller Reminisces,' *Quarterly News-Letter of the Book Club of California*, XXXII:2, Spring 1967.

_____. 'Bookselling in the Mountains,' *Quarterly News-Letter of the Book Club of California*, XIII:3, Spring 1948.

_____. 'The Durham Cathedral Library,' *Quarterly News-Letter of the Book Club of California*, XVIII:2, Spring 1953.

_____. 'Oxford Revisited,' *Quarterly News-Letter of the Book Club of California*, XXIX:3, Summer 1964.

_____. 'Recollections and Prejudices,' *Quarterly News-Letter of the Book Club of California*, XXXIV:4, Fall 1969.

Wheat, Carl I. 'The Roxburghe Club of San Francisco,' *Quarterly News-Letter of the Book Club of California*, XVIII: 2, Spring 1953.

Published in a trade edition
of nine hundred and fifty copies
and in a limited edition of fifty copies,
specially bound and slipcased,
signed and numbered by the author.